Stories for a Woman's Heart

Stories for a Woman's Heart

Over 100 Stories to Encourage Her Soul

COMPILED BY ALICE GRAY

Multnomah® Publishers *Sisters, Oregon*

STORIES FOR A WOMAN'S HEART
published by Multnomah Publishers, Inc.

© 1999 by Multnomah Publishers, Inc.
International Standard Book Number: 1-57673-474-9

Cover image of tea set and interior spot images by Joe Felzman
Cover image of flowers and interior images on section dividers by
Tadashi Ono/Photonica

Printed in the United States of America

Multnomah is a trademark of Multnomah Publishers, Inc.,
and is registered in the U.S. Patent and Trademark Office.
The colophon is a trademark of Multnomah Publishers, Inc.

Stories for the Heart is a trademark of Multnomah Publishers, Inc.,
and is registered in the U.S. Patent and Trademark Office.

Library of Congress Cataloging-in-Publication Data
Stories for a woman's heart: over 100 stories to encourage her soul/
compiled by Alice Gray.   p.cm.   ISBN 1-57673-474-9 (alk. paper)
1. Christian women–Religious life–Anecdotes. 2. Christian women–
conduct of life–Anecdotes. I. Gray, Alice, 1939–
BV4527.S735   1999   98-52834
248.8'43–dc21   CIP

02 03 04 05 — 13 12 11 10 9

Some people come into our lives and quickly go.
Some stay for a while and leave footprints on our hearts.
And we are never, ever the same.

AUTHOR UNKNOWN

To forever friends—

Because of your love,

I will never, ever be the same.

Thank you.

A SPECIAL THANK-YOU—

To Doreen Button, Ruth King, Nancy Larson,

Casandra Lindell, Sandra Snavely, and Sue Thoroughman

who helped me choose stories that celebrate

the wonderful ways of womanhood.

To Kerri Loesche who created peaceful organization

from mounds of chaotic paperwork.

To readers from all over the world

who made my mailbox a cheering section.

Your stories were wonderful.

I wish they all could be included.

To Al Gray

who is the wind beneath my wings.

CONTENTS

Motherhood

Memories

Life

Friendship

❧

MORNING WALK

Six A.M. Two women in windsuits are out for their morning walk. As they walk, they talk about their important friendships: husbands, kids, coworkers. They occasionally touch each other's shoulders, stop, face each other, and laugh. A sun-dried seventy-something man, wearing a neon orange ski hat, walks by, smiles, and says, "You two look like you're doing ballet together." And so they are. As friends, they are dancing in synchrony: listening, encouraging, challenging each other.

AUTHOR UNKNOWN
FROM IN THE COMPANY OF FRIENDS

NORM AND NORMA

Dr. Bettie B. Youngs
FROM *Values From the Heartland*

I will help you," the little boy said, reaching for Norma's tiny hand and placing it in his own. "And I won't let anyone laugh at you no more." We watched, awed by his skills of compassion—uncommon, we thought, for one as young as us.

It was the first day of kindergarten. Too shy to ask the teacher to use the bathroom and too timid to use it without first getting permission, five-year-old Norma sat at her small desk crying because she had wet herself.

It wasn't long before all the other students heard her soft whimpers and began staring in her direction. Some students laughed because they thought her predicament funny; others giggled, no doubt out of relief that it had happened to her and not to them. But one brave little boy did not laugh. Instead, Norm got up from his desk, walked over to his classmate and looking at her, said softly, "I will help you." We were all sitting and he was standing, so his presence seemed almost majestic. "And I won't let them make fun of you," he said reassuringly.

My tiny classmate looked up at Norm and smiled with admiration. His act of kindness had buffered her duress; she no longer felt afraid and alone. She had found a new friend.

Still holding her small hand, the little hero turned, surveyed his class-mates and asked kindly, "How would you feel if it happened to you?" The wise teacher at the head of the classroom observed quietly, but said nothing.

We children sat motionless, stilled partly by the enormous strain and anxiety caused by the drama in this moment, but also because we had just witnessed an act of heroism we had not been able to summon in ourselves. It was a lesson in how precious goodness can be.

Then the little boy added, "Let's not laugh at her anymore, okay?" Intuitively, we knew we were in the presence of courage.

And by his actions, we were persuaded to develop some of our own.

Editor's note: Norma never forgot Norman, nor he her. Their friendship is now celebrating its thirty-sixth year.

> *Be slow in choosing a friend,*
> *Slower in changing.*
> BENJAMIN FRANKLIN

MAY BASKET OF FLOWERS— AND FORGIVENESS

Sue Dunigan
from *Decision* magazine

*H*ey, do you know what? Today is May Day!" my sister announced. "Do you remember the May Day baskets we used to make with colored paper and paste?"

Childhood memories and warm feelings engulfed me as I recalled that my sisters and I would run around our neighborhood delivering the not-so-perfect baskets brimming with spring flowers. We would place the handmade treasures on a doorstep, knock on the door, then scurry away as fast as our legs could carry us. It was delightful to peer around a bush and watch our friends open their doors and pick up the colorful gift, wondering who had left it out for them.

I distinctly remember the May Day of the year that I was in fifth grade. That year I was faced with a challenge involving one of my dearest friends. She lived right across the road from our family, and we had walked together to school nearly every day since first grade.

Pam was a year older than I, however, and her interests were starting to change from the interests that we had had together. A new family had recently moved into our small town, and Pam was spending more and more time at their house. I felt hurt and left out.

When my mother asked me if I was going to take a May Day basket to Pam's house, I responded angrily, "Absolutely not!" My mom stopped what she was doing, knelt down and held me in her arms. She told me not to worry, that I would have many other friends throughout my lifetime.

"But Pam was my very best friend ever," I cried.

Mom smoothed back my hair, wiped away my tears and told me that circumstances change and people change. She explained that one of the greatest things friends can do is to give each other a chance to grow, to change and to develop into all God wants them to be. And sometimes, she said, that would mean that friends would choose to spend time with other people.

She went on to say that I needed to forgive Pam for hurting me—and that I could act out that forgiveness by giving her a May Day basket.

It was a hard decision, but I decided to give her a basket. I made an extra-special basket of flowers with lots of yellow because that was Pam's favorite color. I asked my two sisters to help me deliver my basket of forgiveness. As we watched from our hiding place, Pam scooped up the flowers, pressed her face into them and said loudly enough for us to hear, "Thank you, Susie! I hoped you wouldn't forget me!"

That day I made a decision that changed my life: I decided to hold my friends tightly in my heart, but loosely in my expectations of them, allowing them space to grow and to change—with or without me.

THE TRUEST OF FRIENDS

NANCY SULLIVAN GENG
FROM *GUIDEPOSTS* MAGAZINE

I pulled the pink envelope from our mailbox just as my daughter was coming home from school. It looked like a birthday party invitation. "SARAH" was carefully printed in bold, black letters. When Sarah stepped off the bus I tucked the envelope into her hand. "It's…it's…for me," she stuttered, delighted.

In the unseasonably warm February sun we sat down on the front porch. As I helped her open the envelope, I wondered who had sent it. Maybe Emily or perhaps Michael, pals from her special-education class.

"It's…it's…from Maranda." Sarah said, pointing to the front cover of the card. There, framed with hearts, was a photo of a girl I had never seen before. She had beautiful long hair, a dimpled grin and warm smiling eyes. "Maranda is 8 years old," the caption read. "Come and celebrate on Valentine's Day."

Glancing at the picture, I felt uneasy. Clearly, Maranda was not handicapped. Sarah, on the other hand, had Down's syndrome and was developmentally delayed in all areas. At age nine she still functioned on a preschool level. Her disability was obvious, marked with thick-lensed glasses, a hearing aid and stuttering.

A happy child, she had many friends who used wheelchairs and braces and walkers. But this was the first time she had been invited to the home of a nondisabled child. "How did you meet Maranda?" I asked.

"At...at...school. We eat lunch together every...every day."

Even though Sarah was in special education she socialized with other second graders during gym, lunch and homeroom. I had always hoped she would make friends outside her program. Why, then, did I feel apprehensive?

Because I'm her mother, I thought. I loved Sarah. I wanted and prayed that she would have the best. I also knew a friendship with Sarah called for extra sensitivity, tolerance and understanding. Was the child in the photo capable of that?

Valentine's Day came. Sarah dressed in her favorite pink lace dress and white patent leather shoes. As we drove to Maranda's party she sat next to me in the front seat, clutching the Barbie doll she had wrapped with Winnie-the-Pooh paper and masking tape. "I...I'm so excited," she said.

I smiled, but deep inside I felt hesitant. There would be other children at the party. Would they tease Sarah? Would Maranda be embarrassed in front of her other friends? *Please, Lord,* I prayed, *don't let Sarah get hurt.*

I pulled into the driveway of a house decorated with silver heart-shaped balloons. Waiting at the front door was a little girl in a red sweater trimmed with ribboned hearts. It was Maranda. "Sarah's here!" she called. Racing to our car, she welcomed my daughter with a wraparound hug. Soon seven giggling girls followed Maranda's lead, welcoming Sarah with smiles.

"Bye, Mom," Sarah said, waving as she and the others ran laughing into the house. Maranda's mother, Mary, greeted me at my rolled-down car window.

"Thanks for bringing Sarah," she said. Mary went on to explain that her daughter was an only child and that Maranda and Sarah had become special friends at school. "Maranda talks about her all the time," she said.

I drove away, amazed. Still, I couldn't get over my uneasiness. Could this friendship ever be equal? Maranda would need to learn the language of Sarah's speech. She would need patience when Sarah struggled with certain tasks. That was a lot to ask of an eight year old.

As the months passed, I watched the girls' friendship grow. They spent many hours together in our home. Fixing dinner in the kitchen, I heard giggles fill the family room as they twirled around an old recliner or watched *The Lion King*. Other times they dressed up in my old hats and outdated blouses, pretending to be famous singers.

One afternoon in late autumn, I watched the two of them sitting next to each other at our kitchen table. Sarah held a pencil; Maranda had a tablet of paper.

Maranda called out each letter as she guided Sarah's hand: "S-A-R-A-H." Though some of the letters had been printed backwards or upside down, Maranda praised Sarah's effort. "Great job," she said, applauding.

At Christmastime the girls exchanged gifts. Sarah gave Maranda a photograph of herself, a framed first-communion picture. "You look beautiful," Maranda said as she admired Sarah's white ruffled dress and long lace veil. In return, Maranda gave Sarah a gray-flannel elephant trimmed with an "I love you" tag. It quickly became Sarah's favorite stuffed animal, and she slept with it every night.

A few weeks into the new school year Sarah came home from school looking downcast. "M-Maranda is…is sick," she said. I thought maybe she had caught the bug circulating at school. Minutes later, however, Sarah's special-education teacher called. Maranda was in the hospital. She had sustained a seizure at school and had been diagnosed with a brain tumor. Surgeons had performed a risky operation, which had left Maranda paralyzed on one side with impaired speech and vision. The biopsy results weren't back yet.

"Can we visit her?" I asked. I knew Sarah would want to see her friend.

"Maranda is very despondent and not up to seeing anybody," the teacher told me. "Her parents are requesting cards rather than visitors."

"We'll keep her in our prayers," I promised.

That night Sarah knelt beside her bed, clutching her stuffed elephant. "Please ma…ma…make Maranda better," she prayed. Night after night she implored God to heal her friend. Then one night in early February, Sarah stopped abruptly in the middle of her prayer. She nudged me.

"Let's ma…ma…make a valentine for Ma……Maranda."

The next day we sat together at the kitchen table as I helped Sarah write Maranda's name on a large sheet of pink-and-white construction paper. She decorated each letter with stickers and glittery Magic Markers. She drew a large heart around the name, then glued candy hearts with phrases like "friends forever" and "be mine." In similar fashion she added four more pages. Just before we slid the card into a large envelope, Sarah asked, "How…how…how do I spell love?" I called out the letters as she painstakingly printed "LOVE," the letters crooked and out of place, followed by her name.

Two weeks passed. We heard that Maranda had additional surgery. On Valentine's Day I got a phone call from her mother. "Maranda's home," she said, "and wants to see Sarah."

"Home?" I asked with surprise.

"Maranda's tumor was benign. We're hoping for a full recovery."

As we discussed Maranda's prognosis, she relayed how thankful she was for Sarah and her card. "Maranda was very depressed. She had stacks of letters, cards and gifts but wouldn't open any of them. Then one morning Sarah's homemade card arrived. We opened it and Maranda burst into a huge smile. She hugged it and wouldn't put it down," Mary's voice was choked with emotion. "It was an answer to prayer."

I realized then that Sarah and Maranda were the truest of friends. Their bond was defined not by intellect or health or handicap, but by love, unconditionally given and received. They had overcome disability with laughter and support. Their friendship had always been equal.

Today both girls are doing well. Maranda is almost 12 and Sarah is going on 13. With the help of intensive therapy Maranda's neurological functions returned to normal, and Sarah's speech has improved immensely. She can even read some. Though we've moved to a different neighborhood, the girls still keep in touch. Recently Maranda came to a sleepover.

As the girls sat at our kitchen table, they talked about Maranda's newly pierced ears and Sarah's "secret" boyfriend from her special-ed class. Then in the middle of their conversation, Sarah opened a kitchen drawer and pulled out a tablet and pencil.

"S-A-R-A-H," Maranda called out, just like old times. As Sarah printed her name without any help, Maranda looked on and clapped. "Great job, Sarah!" she said. I took a peek at my daughter's masterpiece. Her name had been written perfectly.

FRIENDS NEVER FORGET

I think of my women friends as a raft we make with our arms. We are out there in the middle of some great scary body of water, forearm to forearm, hand to elbow, holding tight. Sometimes I am part of the raft, joining up with others to provide safe harbor; other times I need to climb aboard myself, until the storms subside and I can see my way clear to swim to shore. The raft drifts apart when it's not needed, but never disbands, never forgets.

BEVERLY LOWREY
SELF MAGAZINE

New Friends

*U*pon arriving in our new home in Kentucky, my seven-year-old son Jason decided to explore the neighborhood. He was back within the hour proclaiming that he had made some new friends.

"Good. Are they boys or girls?" I asked.

"One is a boy and one is a girl," he replied.

"That's great," I said. "How old are they?"

"Mom," my son replied, almost shocked. "That would be very rude to ask."

I was puzzled at his response. About an hour later, he was back.

"Mom!" my son shouted through the screen door. "I found out how old my new friends are. The girl is 65 and the boy is 70."

TERI LEINBAUGH
FROM *THE CHRISTIAN READER*

THE FRONT PORCH CLASSROOM

PHILIP GULLEY
FROM *FRONT PORCH TALES*

When I was in the fourth grade, I was offered a job as a paperboy. It didn't pay much money, but I knew having a job would build my character so I took it, good character being important to fourth-graders. My lessons started the first day on the job. A customer paying his bill asked me if I wanted a tip, and I said, "Sure." He said, "Stay away from wild women."

One of my customers was a lady named Mrs. Stanley. She was a widow and not prone to wild living, so I took to lingering on her front porch during my rounds. She'd watch for me to come down her street, and by the time I'd pedaled up to her house, there'd be a slushy bottle of Coke waiting for me. I'd sit and drink while she talked. That was our understanding—I drank, she talked.

The widow Stanley talked mostly about her dead husband, Roger. "Roger and I went grocery shopping this morning over to the IGA," she'd say. The first time she said that, the Coke went up my nose. That was back in the days when Coke going up your nose wasn't a crime, just a mite uncomfortable.

Went home and told my father about Mrs. Stanley and how she talked as if Mr. Stanley were still alive. Dad said she was probably lonely, and that maybe I just ought to sit and listen and nod my head and smile, and maybe she'd work it out of her system. So that's what I did. I figured this was where the character-building came into play. Turned out Dad was right. After a few summers, she seemed content to leave her husband over at the South Cemetery.

Nowadays, we'd send Mrs. Stanley to a psychiatrist. But all she had back then was a front porch rocker and her paperboy's ear, which turned out to be enough.

I quit my paper route after her healing. Moved on to the lucrative business of lawn mowing. Didn't see the widow Stanley for several years. Then we crossed paths up at the Christian Church's annual fund-raiser dinner. She was standing behind the steam table spooning out mashed potatoes and looking radiant. Four years ago she'd had to bribe her paperboy with a Coke to have someone to talk with; now she had friends brimming over. Her husband was gone, but life went on. She had her community and was luminous with love.

Community is a beautiful thing; sometimes it even heals us and makes us better than we would otherwise be.

I live in the city now. My front porch is a concrete slab. And my paperboy is a lady named Edna with three kids and a twelve-year-old Honda. Every day she asks me how I'm doing. When I don't say "fine," she sticks around long enough to find out why. She's such a nice lady that sometimes I act as if I have a problem, just so she'll tarry. She's lived in the city all her life, but she knows about community, too.

Community isn't so much a locale as it is a state of mind. You find it whenever folks ask how you're doing because they care, and not because they're getting paid to inquire.

Two thousand years ago, a church elder named Peter wrote the recipe for community. "Above all else," he wrote, "hold unfailing your love for one another, since love covers a multitude of sins" (1 Peter 4:8). That means when you love a person, you occasionally have to turn a blind eye toward their shortcomings.

Kind of like what my dad told me about the widow Stanley. Sometimes it's better to nod your head and smile.

Psychiatrists call that "enabling denial," but back when I delivered papers, we called it "compassion."

FRIENDSHIP

Oh,
The comfort—
The inexpressible comfort
Of feeling safe with a person,
Having neither to weigh thoughts,
Nor measure words, but pouring them all right
out, just as they are, chaff and grain together,
Certain that a faithful hand will take and sift
them, keep what is worth keeping—
And with a breath of kindness,
Blow the rest
away.

DINAH MARIE MULOCK CRAIK

AMY DAYS

LISA LATHAM GREEN
FROM *WELCOME HOME* MAGAZINE

I've known Amy since kindergarten. She's been my best friend since second grade. Amy taught me long division. We were confirmed at the same time and were attendants at each other's weddings one summer. We went to graduate school and even bought our first houses simultaneously—houses with similar gigantic Los Angeles mortgages.

Through letters we kept tabs on our hopes and dreams, and when I learned of her pregnancy through a Christmas card, I immediately called to tell her of mine. We'd both been afraid to phone our news—afraid of somehow crushing the other with our good fortune.

I was due twenty-five days before Amy, committed to natural childbirth the Bradley way. Amy had chosen Lamaze. When she called me on the day before my due date, I said that I was in labor and it was sweet of her to call and check on me. She softly replied that she was calling to announce the birth of her daughter, Rebecca Anne, the day before.

Emily Catherine was born the following day, making our first children both girls, born two days apart. Emily's christening, an intimate affair including Amy and her tiny family, was scheduled a month later. It was the first time we'd seen each other in over two months. Amy had lost her baby weight. I hadn't. Since Amy had a few months before she had to return to work, she suggested that we get together. I agreed and called the next day. Thus began my "Amy Days."

Amy Days were special. They were canceled only for illness. Weekly, we alternated driving the thirty-two miles in Los Angeles traffic—one-and-a-half hours one way, but it was worth it. On Amy Days the dishes and laundry waited until I returned. I left with a light heart, a full diaper bag, and a smile. I would return, exhausted from the drive (about half an hour from home, Emily and I would get stuck in a traffic jam that usually provoked her to cry the rest of the way), but I would be renewed, ready to tackle the next week of mothering.

We planned outings to the library, buggy rides around our neighbor-hoods, photo sessions with still and video cameras, and excursions to the mall for makeovers. We designed matching Christmas playsuits, carefully sewing to fit growing babies. But mostly we just played with our children and talked.

My husband's job has taken us to Austin, Texas, fifteen hundred miles from Amy, but we still stay in touch. Through phone calls, Amy and I have shared the scariness of bronchitis, the trials of potty training, and the joy we have in our blossoming children. And though my Amy Days are now mere phone calls at odd hours, they are no less important to the fabric of my life.

LITTLE MOMMIES ALONG THE WAY

CASANDRA LINDELL

The letter was short and cut right to the point. I had never been so viciously attacked by someone I thought was a close friend. Crying, I called Sue. We had met as students and she had quickly become like a sister to me.

"What's going on?" she asked right away.

"I got a letter. Can I come over there?"

"Absolutely."

I sobbed all the way to her house as the words from the letter swirled through my mind, cutting deeper with each circle. I didn't understand the accusations. The confusion added to my pain.

When I arrived, I simply handed her the letter without a word and sat on the couch to watch her read it. Her face moved from curiosity to confusion, through pain to outrage as she sat stroking the fluffy orange cat curled in her lap. Many times, she sighed and shook her head. That in itself was comforting: I had been afraid the words of the letter might be true.

Then, Sue folded the pages she held. As she stood, she scooped up the cat in one arm and a quilt in the other. "I don't know where this person is coming from, but I do know this."

She spread the quilt over my lap. "You need a blankey."

She dropped the cat on top of the quilt. "And you need a kitty."

She sat next to me, put her arm around my shoulder, and pulled my head against her. "And you need a mommy. Go ahead and cry." Lovingly, she absorbed pain from me as my tears kept coming. The cat purred in my lap. The quilt warmed me. My friend held me tight. To this day, I feel the comfort of that scene.

Another friend of mine calls tender moments like these "little mommies." No matter how old we get, we never stop needing a mom, even when she isn't there. Some mothers were never nurturing, some may be out when we call, and some are no longer with us. But each of us still needs a "little mommy" along the way from the people in our lives who care for us.

A friend is...
Someone who understands your past
Believes in your future
And accepts you just the way you are.

AUTHOR UNKNOWN

THE HANDS OF FRIENDS

JANE KIRKPATRICK
FROM *A BURDEN SHARED*

A winter wind whipped past her through the parlor door. Before her, women sat and stitched. Their worn and wrinkled fingers pulled together pieces of her past cut into little squares: a child's worn dress, a bedroom curtain, a flowered tablecloth (with the berry stain her husband made one holiday cut out and now discarded). Dozens of memories they patched together.

That day the women did the final stitching, making perfect edges then tying the tiny strings to keep the stuffing behind each quilted piece. They sewed the single-colored backing down. The comforter, completed, would keep her warm through winter's winds.

What comforts are the memories, the patches that mark the past and then are held together with the stitching hands of friends placed over solid backing. Surrounded by the fondness, we recall the memories, let them nourish us, keep us warm, and give us much needed sleep; knowing in the morning we can set aside the quilt, rested, still wrapped in comfort.

In these difficult days, I give my comforter to you. May the memories you wish to savor wrap themselves around you, stitched together by the hands of friends.

THE GIFT OF GAB

LYNN ROGERS PETRAK

*A*lthough she told me not to talk to strangers, my mother always did. At the checkout line. Browsing through handbags at Marshall Field. During a slow elevator ride, when everyone else was seriously squinting at the buttons. At airports, football games and the beach.

Thankfully, I only took her advice when it came to menacing strangers. I believe I'm better for it.

My mother's habit of striking up conversations with people next to her may bring a smile to my eyes now, but it proved rather embarrassing during my tender teenage years. "Lynn's getting her first one, too," she confided to a woman also shopping with her adolescent daughter in the bra section of our hometown department store. I contemplated running and hiding under a nearby terry cloth bathrobe, but instead I turned crimson and hissed "Mothhhhherrrrr" between gritted teeth. I felt only slightly better when the girl's mother said, "We're trying to find one for Sarah, but they're all too big."

Not everyone responded when Mom made an observation and tried to spark a brief discussion. Some people gave her a tight-lipped half-grin, then turned away. A few completely ignored her. Whenever I was with her during those times, I could see that she was a little hurt, but she'd shrug it off and we'd continue on our way.

More often than not, however, I would wander off somewhere and come back to find her gabbing away. There were occasions when I was concerned that I'd lost her in the crowd, but then I'd hear her singsong laugh and a comment like, "Yes, yes, me too."

Through these spontaneous chats, my mother taught me that our world is much too large—or too small, take your pick—not to have time to reach out to one another. She reminded me that as women, we enjoy a special kind of kinship, even if we're really not all that alike. In the most mundane things, there are common threads that bind us. It may be the reason we like paper versus plastic, or why a navy sweater is never a bad buy, or why the national anthem still gives us goose bumps.

One of the last memories of my mother, when she was in the hospital and a few hours from dying from the breast cancer that had ravaged her down to 85 pounds, is of her smiling weakly and talking to her nurse about how to best plant tulip bulbs. I stood silently in the doorway, wanting to cry but feeling such a surge of love and warmth. She taught me to see spring in others. I'll never forget it, especially now when I turn to someone and say, "Don't you just love it when…"

DIAL A FRIEND

SUSAN SCHOENBERGER
FROM *THE BALTIMORE SUN* MAGAZINE

A list hangs on my refrigerator, anchored by a bagel-shaped magnet. I could take it down, since the phone numbers are memorized, but I keep it there for comfort. It's a remarkable list, really, reminding me that life is unpredictable, and not always in a bad way. Somebody has to win the lottery.

One day in the summer of '92, when my son was six months old, I got a letter. It was handwritten, the kind you get only often enough to keep you sorting through the junk mail. I read it three times.

The writer, A. J. Blye, was a mother of two who recently had moved to Baltimore from California. She'd gotten our name and address from the diaper service we used, she said, and she had an idea.

Looking back, I'm surprised my cynical self didn't suspect A. J. of organizing a kidnapping ring. But the letter struck just the right note: I was on maternity leave and was beginning to realize how tough it was to make new friends who'd want to spend time watching me mix up rice cereal. I've never been one of those people who can knock on doors and introduce themselves, striking up lifelong friendships.

But A. J. was.

So my husband and I walked a few blocks to her house one Saturday and met seven neighborhood couples who all had children still in diapers. In a few hours we put together a baby-sitting co-op and agreed to a regular Friday-evening exchange in which two couples would watch all the kids while the other six couples went out.

I came away with my list.

At first the numbers—as unfamiliar as the people on the other end of the line—had no personality. So I was a little nervous about dialing, afraid I would call at a bad time or reach someone who wasn't quite sure this co-op thing was a good idea.

In a way, we trusted each other before we really knew each other. Moreover, I sensed that people willing to share their children with me probably could be trusted with mine. But the friendships took time.

Every Friday evening I learned more about the names on my list as we broke up rumbles over toys or went out together on our off days. The numbers became familiar, almost dialing themselves, and all the kids and mothers became something special—the kind of extended family I didn't have nearby.

The list changed my life. I realized that while having lunch with three other mothers and four children one summer day. Pieces of hot dog and french fries littered the floor as we talked about books, movies and teething. I realized that I would have liked these people as friends regardless of whether they had children.

When I look at the juice-stained paper under the bagel magnet now, I see what anchors me to the neighborhood. I've moved around quite a bit since college—five cities in nine years—and none of them felt like home. But what made my mother's house a home? It wasn't the framed photographs or the piano or the fireplace. It was the phone numbers she could call whenever she needed a friend to plan a party, to give one of her four children a lift or just yak into the night.

There is power in my list, power in its ready feedback and in the confidence it gives me. If I have a party, someone will come.

There was a time when such a list would have compiled itself, as people grew up in their respective neighborhoods, settled down and had children. And grandparents probably would have been nearby, ready to offer a weekly night out.

But that's increasingly rare today. Of the 16 adults in our group, only two grew up in Baltimore and still have family there.

So the list, always tacked on the fridge, has taken on that role. It means I'm home.

(Reprinted with permission from the February 1998 *Reader's Digest*)

THE SONG

I breathed a song into the air,
It fell to earth
I know not where…
And the song,
from beginning to end,
I found again
in the heart of a friend.

HENRY WADSWORTH LONGFELLOW

MOVING DAY

DORIS HIER
FROM *THE CHRISTIAN READER*

y friend Jeri threw a few remaining odds and ends into the last box. This was one moving day she was not excited about. There was nothing wrong with the house, except it was on the "other side of town." Friends cautioned them about always locking their doors, something they'd never been in the habit of doing before.

When moving day arrived, the helpers all remembered to secure the house between loads—until the last load! Someone had forgotten to lock the door. Cautiously, they entered the house discovering that someone had indeed invaded their home in that short interval of time.

The intruders had left a calling card. There on the kitchen counter stood a pot of freshly brewed coffee, a chocolate cake, and a big pot of chili, complete with everything needed for a "welcome to the neighborhood" meal.

THE FINE ART
OF WAVING

JOËL FREEMAN
FROM *COUNTRY LIVING* MAGAZINE

*M*y husband will wave to anyone. He attributes this tendency to a span of time he spent on a small island off the coast of Rhode Island. There, the only people who didn't wave to you in passing were tourists—and you certainly didn't want to be accused of being one of those. Besides, he feels that waving is an act of goodwill and that even the grumpiest person will feel a little better after being greeted by a hearty wave.

That's why, when we moved from a house in the woods to a house on a main road, we continued our custom of waving whenever a familiar car drove by. A sense of neighborliness required us to do so.

My husband and I take turns standing in front of our house with our second-grader as she waits for the school bus. Every day, the same people drive by on their way to work or school. There is the small pink vehicle we call the Barbie car, for example, and the circa 1970s van covered with gray patches of body filler that we refer to as the Hippiemobile. Some drivers give us a big smile and wave like we've known one another all our lives. Others start out tentatively, moving their hand only slightly so that if we don't wave back they can pretend they were only fixing their hair or scratching their forehead.

I understand their hesitation. Unlike my spouse, I can't bring myself to wave to everyone. Once, while we were on one of our exploring jaunts, we found an appealing back road that turned out to be a good shortcut to a lake. We had to slow down considerably to negotiate a sharp curve. Just beyond the bend, we were surprised by an elderly woman sitting in a green lawn chair situated directly on the side of the road. As we passed her, she waved. It turns out she sits there every day and waves to every car that happens to go by. I have always felt she must be a little eccentric or lonely. But this is reading a lot into the situation, because she looks very contented. Anyway, a part of me fears that people will think I am eccentric if I start waving to every car that goes by our house. After all, I am home a great deal more than my husband is!

You probably would be surprised, though, to discover how many people wave to us first now. Some people accompany the gesture with a toot of their horn, which is the heartiest kind of wave. Friends from town that come to visit us and relax with us on our front porch soon find themselves automatically raising their hand in salute to passersby. I always tell these congenial guests that they have just learned the fine art of waving.

Yesterday I went to the post office. In the lobby, standing in front of me in line, was a man I have waved to almost daily for the past four years. He heard my toddler babbling behind him and turned around to look.

"How you all doing? Boy, this one sure is getting big!" he said to me, smiling at my child.

"She surely is! I have to watch her every minute," I replied.

"I'll bet. Hey, that new deck looks great!"

"Thanks—we love it."

"Well, have a great day—nice seeing you."

"You, too! Bye-bye."

The funny thing is, we had never met before.

SURPRISE IN THE PARK

SARA (CANDY) DUBOSE
FROM *SUNDAY DIGEST*

*L*ike a magnet, the gentle warmth of the afternoon sun was already drawing Sara outside when her eight- and ten-year-old daughters came to her with their request.

"Please, Mama, could we go to the park?"

"Sure, why not?" Sara answered, a smile crinkling her eyes.

After packing a few snacks, they were off. The giant oaks and hickories in Oak Park were a perfect setting—a place to play, think, and let your soul have a beauty soak.

Soon DeAnn and Cherie were telling Sara where to stop, a place near their favorite swings and climbing bars. As she sat on a nearby bench watching her two acrobats, Sara somehow felt this was going to be a special day, a day of adventure and discovery.

It wasn't long before a young boy about nine ran down to join in the fun. At first, there was the usual "you do your thing and I'll do mine" kind of action, but after a time they began taking turns pushing each other and playing tag. Sara didn't catch any of their conversation but they all appeared to be enjoying a glorious summer day. Pleased that her daughters were having fun with a new friend, Sara propped up her paperback book and began to read.

"Mama," DeAnn called, "can you come down here a minute?"

Sighing, Sara slipped the book back in her purse and headed for the sandy play area. Each child was holding a long stick and DeAnn pointed to a message scribbled in the sand. In large letters it read: "I can't hear or talk, but my name is Dan."

Under Dan, DeAnn and Cherie had both carefully spelled out their names. The children all looked very serious as Dan held his broken branch to Sara.

Trying not to overreact, Sara took it and wrote Mom under her daughters' names. A big smile broke out on Dan's face—a smile that seemed to come from deep inside.

For a moment they all just stood there looking down into the sand. Then a thought struck Sara. Above the four names there was enough room for one more. Sara took Dan's stick again and wrote God. Then she pointed up to the sky.

Dan grinned again, his eyes shining. He nodded, then pointed heavenward and to his heart. Still not satisfied that his message was complete, Dan took the stick back and drew a huge circle around the names and then reached over to touch each person.

It was beautiful. Four people—all children really—and all in the circle of a caring God. It was indeed a day of adventure and discovery.

BUT I DON'T
HAVE ANYONE!

SUSAN ALEXANDER YATES AND ALLISON YATES GASKINS
FROM *THANKS, MOM, FOR EVERYTHING*

*I*t was Mother's Day. A day for celebrating, a day for honoring, and a day when your children overlook your faults and tell you how great you are. A day to honor the mothers in your own life.

It should have been a day of rejoicing. But for Jay and Heather sitting alone in the restaurant, it was a sad reminder of losses. Already in their late forties, they had given up any hope of having children. On this day Heather especially felt the loss that her barrenness represented. Watching a young family at the next table giving their mother gifts didn't help any.

"It just doesn't seem fair," she murmured, while picking at her food. "They are so happy because they have someone."

Her husband, Jay, tried to cheer her up but he too felt a sense of loss. He had had a difficult year watching his mother die. She had been the last of their parents to go, and now they were all alone with no children of their own to comfort them.

Maybe taking Heather out wasn't such a good idea after all, he thought. *Probably we should have just stayed at home.*

Leaning back on his chair Jay began to glance around the room. His eyes came to rest on a table in the corner. Two elderly women sat quietly eating their salads. One in particular made Jay's heart skip a beat. Wispy white curls framed a slightly pudgy face with a long straight nose. Startled, Jay though of how much the old woman's profile reminded him of his own mother's. And then he noticed her companion. She too was elderly.

"Heather," he said, "look at those two women eating alone. They are about the same ages our moms would be if they were alive. I wonder if they have any children?"

Glancing at the women, Heather was silent for a moment.

"They do look awfully alone," she said. "I wonder...."

Suddenly, Heather's face lit up. "Jay," she said, "let's pay for their dinners. But let's not let them know. It can be our Mother's Day gift to them."

Enthusiastic with the change in his wife's mood, Jay called the waitress over and explained that they wanted to pay for the women's dinner in honor of Mother's Day but that it must be anonymous.

Their waitress agreed to help with this special surprise, and Jay and Heather sat back to watch what would happen next. When the women called for their bill, they were told that it was a Mother's Day gift from someone anonymous who wanted to honor them. Shock and pleasure showed in their wrinkled faces as Jay and Heather watched from a few tables away.

But these women were insistent; they had to know.

"Who would do such a kind thing?" they asked.

Finally the poor waitress could no longer keep the secret, and nodding in Jay and Heather's direction she gave the secret away.

Quickly the women made their way over to Jay and Heather's table. Profusely thanking the couple, they asked if they might join them at their table. As introductions were given and stories were shared, a special friendship was begun, one that was to continue throughout the year. This friendship grew and one year later, on Mother's Day, Jay and Heather brought their new "moms" to dinner for a "family" celebration!

Love

CALLING LONG DISTANCE

I read about one man who called his wife from an airport pay phone. When he had used up all his coins, the operator interrupted to say he had one minute left. The man hurriedly tried to finish his conversation with his wife, but before they could tell each other good-bye, the line went dead. With a sigh, the man hung up the phone and started to leave the little telephone cubicle. Just then the phone rang. Thinking it was the operator wanting more money, the man almost didn't answer. But something told him to pick up the phone. And sure enough, it was the operator. But she didn't want more money. Instead she had a message for him.

"After you hung up, your wife said she loved you," the operator said. "I thought you'd want to know."

BARBARA JOHNSON
FROM *WE BRAKE FOR JOY!*

IN A CATHEDRAL OF FENCEPOSTS AND HARLEYS

Neil Parker

I have had only two rules to guide which weddings I will do, and which I will turn down: I need to be able to meet with the bride and groom first, and I don't do weddings in unusual places—like parachuting or underwater.

But I broke both rules once, and it was the most meaningful wedding I ever celebrated.

I'd agreed to do this wedding on two days' notice when the minister who was to officiate was unavailable due to a family emergency. I had the details of the location (well out of town, on a farm); I knew the names of the bride and groom; and I knew that they'd done pre-marital sessions with the other minister.

I also knew something about their wedding guests and the particular setting they'd chosen for the celebration of their union. One hundred and forty bikers had come up to spend the weekend. And the wedding was to be an added bonus—and a surprise to all but a handful of the guests.

I confess to considerable misgivings as I turned off the highway onto the property and caught my first glimpse of the venue. Dozens of motorcycles filled the parking lot. Most were Harley-Davidsons, the choice of serious bikers. Very loud music filled the air from a tent and refreshment area in the center field. Tents dotted the landscape. It looked like a heavy-metal Woodstock.

Mine was the only Jetta in sight. I parked it and headed up to the house.

At least, to my relief, things seemed to be in order there. I was introduced to the bride's parents and the groom's parents while the bride was getting dressed. It didn't take long; jeans and a black T-shirt needed little more than a few flowers in the hair. The groom was introduced to me as "Bear." It wasn't hard to know where the nickname came from; Bear outweighed me at least two to one. His beard was thick and bushy, and his arms were heavily tattooed. Bear didn't say much.

Once we'd checked to see that the license was in order and everything was ready, I headed down to the big tent. I don't push through crowds very well, meek and mild sort that I am, but I managed to get to the front, asked for a microphone, waited for the music to go silent, introduced myself, and announced that I was here for a wedding. I wasn't quite sure what reaction I was going to get.

Several of the bikers immediately headed to the parking lot. The air was filled with the throb of powerful engines revving. Then, with almost military precision, the bikes streamed out of the parking lot and straight toward the center field, heading directly toward me. A few feet away, they turned off to form a double row facing each other—an honor guard to create an aisle for the bride. With engines at full throttle, their roar echoed across the valley.

As the bride walked slowly and gracefully down this aisle, each bike she passed switched off its engine. As she passed the last pair, and all the engines were stilled, you could have heard a pin drop. She walked shyly up to Bear. His eyes were overflowing with tears. Then the birds started to sing.

All around the host couple were the congregation of their friends, members and families of the Sober Riders, each one a recovering alcoholic, each one a biker. Each one was bowed in prayer as we entered a holy moment.

The bride had given me only one instruction for the service. "Make sure you have a sermon," she said. "These people want to hear a word from God."

Her people. And, for an afternoon, my people. I stood in the middle of the field, in a congregation of T-shirts, jeans, and tattoos, in front of a groom and bride who knew exactly what they were doing and why, in a cathedral of fenceposts and Harleys, and we gave thanks to God together.

WEDDING PLANS

My fiancé and I met with our pastor to discuss our upcoming wedding. I wanted an outdoor wedding, but I was hesitant to mention it since a church setting seemed more "official."

My concern was quickly eased by the pastor's response.

"Oh, you'll still be married in a sanctuary," he assured us. "The ceiling will just be a little higher."

GAYLE URBAN
FROM *THE CHRISTIAN READER*

MUSIC OF LOVE

CORRIE FRANZ COWART

Sometimes we find threads of life that bind generation to generation. Sometimes there are symbols that make family history alive in the present. When I sit down to play my grandfather's piano I feel this thrill. I hear him playing evening lullabies to my mother, passionate Beethoven for my grandmother, and playful jigs for me to dance to. Grandfather Lester's piano is a symbol of abiding love.

The son of a small-town preacher, Lester was not born into great worldly wealth. Rather than money, he received a virtuous upbringing in which he learned the values of self-reliance and undying resolve, and found his joy in the creative aspects of life. Captivated by his love of music, Lester chopped cords of wood to earn lesson time with the piano teacher.

The Depression meant an end to Grandfather Lester's college education, as well as his musical pursuits. He was thirty when he married his sweetheart, Frances, and the two of them began to make the sweet domestic harmony of a little home and family.

Lester's interest in music never subsided. Whenever he could, he listened to and studied the great classical composers. He didn't, however, have much of an opportunity to practice his own talents. With many bills to be paid and the prospect of children on the way, purchasing a piano for himself just was not practical or realistic.

In 1942 he was drafted and sent to the European front lines. Every day, amid the horrors of war, Lester found time to write to his dearest Frances. He longed to be home with her and the "little man," the name he gave their newborn son, in the "little mansion," the title he bestowed on their modest home. His cherished correspondence, carefully preserved, was read and reread, as every day Frances would anxiously await his next letter.

Lester sent all the money he could to support his young family, while Frances worked part time as a nurse to help make ends meet. Scrimping and saving, she lived on the bare necessities, praying continually for her husband's safety.

Then one day in March 1946, with the war over and Europe finally secured, Lester returned to his family in the "little mansion." To his surprise a gift of love awaited him. All the checks he had sent to feed his small family had been carefully saved to buy a gift to feed his soul. Frances, forgoing comfort for herself, had saved nearly every penny to buy a piano for her beloved husband. It was just a small spinet, but to Lester it could not look or sound better than the world's finest concert grand.

Though Grandpa Lester and Grandma Frances have passed from this earth, every note from this instrument sings of my grandparents' love for one another and their love for me still. It is music that connects across seas, through generations and beyond death.

MARTHA'S SECRET INGREDIENT

ROY J. REIMAN
FROM *REMINISCE* MAGAZINE

*I*t bothered Ben every time he went through the kitchen. It was that little metal container on the shelf above Martha's cookstove. He probably would not have noticed it so much or been bothered by it if Martha had not repeatedly told him never to touch it. The reason, she said, was that it contained a "secret herb" from her mother, and since she had no way of ever refilling the container, she was concerned that if Ben or anyone else ever picked it up and looked inside, they might accidentally drop it and spill its valuable contents.

The container wasn't really much to look at. It was so old that much of its original red and gold floral colors had faded. You could tell right where it had been gripped again and again as the container was lifted and its tight lid pulled off.

Not only Martha's fingers had gripped it there, but her mother's and her grandmother's had, too. Martha didn't know for sure, but she felt that perhaps even her great-grandmother had used this same container and its "secret herb."

All Ben knew for sure was that shortly after he'd married Martha, her mother had brought the container to Martha and told her to make the same loving use of its contents as she had.

And she did, faithfully. Ben never saw Martha cook a dish without taking the container off the shelf and sprinkling just a little of the "secret herb" over the ingredients. Even when she baked cakes, pies and cookies, he saw her add a light sprinkling just before she put the pans in the oven.

Whatever was in that container, it sure worked, for Ben felt Martha was the best cook in the world. He wasn't alone in that opinion—anyone who ever ate at their house grandly praised Martha's cooking.

But why wouldn't she let Ben touch that little container? Was she really afraid he'd spill its contents? And what did that "secret herb" look like? It was so fine that whenever Martha sprinkled it over the food she was preparing, Ben couldn't quite make out its texture. She obviously had to use very little of it because there was no way of refilling the container.

Somehow Martha had stretched those contents over 30 years of marriage to date. It never failed to effect mouth-watering results.

Ben became increasingly tempted to look into that container just once, but never brought himself to do so.

Then one day Martha became ill. Ben took her to the hospital, where they kept her overnight. When he returned home, he found it extremely lonely in the house. Martha had never been gone overnight before. And when it neared supper time, he wondered what to do—Martha had so loved to cook, he'd never bothered to learn much about preparing food.

As he wandered into the kitchen to see what might be in the refrigerator, the container on the shelf immediately came into view. His eyes were drawn to it like a magnet—he quickly looked away, but his curiosity drew him back.

Curiosity nagged.

What was in that container? Why wasn't he to touch it? What did that "secret herb" look like? How much of it was left?

Ben looked away again and lifted the cover of a large cake pan on the kitchen counter. Ahh...there was more than half of one of Martha's great cakes left over. He cut off a large piece, sat down at the kitchen table, and hadn't taken more than one bite when his eyes went back to that container again. What would it hurt if he looked inside? Why was Martha so secretive about that container, anyway?

Ben took another bite and debated with himself—should he or shouldn't he? For five more big bites he thought about it, staring at the container. Finally he could no longer resist.

He walked slowly across the room and ever so carefully took the container off the shelf—fearing that, horror of horrors, he'd spill the contents while sneaking a peek.

He set the container on the counter and carefully pried off the lid. He was almost scared to look inside! When the inside of the container came into full view, Ben's eyes opened wide—why, the container was empty...except for a little folded slip of paper at the bottom.

Ben reached down for the paper, his big rugged hand struggling to get inside. He carefully picked it up by a corner, removed it and slowly unfolded it under the kitchen light.

A brief note was scrawled inside, and Ben immediately recognized the handwriting as that of Martha's mother. Very simply it said: "Martha—To everything you make, add a dash of love."

Ben swallowed hard, replaced the note and the container, and quietly went back to finishing his cake. Now he completely understood why it tasted so good.

Love one another deeply from the heart.

1 PETER 1:22

LOVE WITHOUT A NET

❧

CHARLES R. SWINDOLL
FROM *GROWING STRONG IN THE SEASONS OF LIFE*

*A*nne Morrow was shy and delicate. Butterfly like. Not dull or stupid or incompetent, just a quiet specimen of timidity. Her dad was ambassador to Mexico when she met an adventurous young fellow who visited south of the border for the U.S. State Department. The man was flying from place to place promoting aviation. Everywhere he went he drew capacity crowds. You see, he had just won $40,000 for being the first to cross the Atlantic by air. The strong pilot and the shy princess fell deeply in love.

When she became Mrs. Charles Lindbergh, Anne could have easily been eclipsed by her husband's shadow. She wasn't however. The love that bound the two together for the next forty-seven years was tough love, mature love, tested by triumph and tragedy alike. They would never know the quiet comfort of being an anonymous couple in a crowd. The Lindbergh name didn't allow that luxury. Her man, no matter where he went, was news, forever in the limelight…clearly a national hero. But rather than becoming a resentful recluse or another nameless face in a crowd of admirers, Anne Morrow Lindbergh emerged to become one of America's most popular authors, a woman highly admired for her own accomplishments.

How? Let's let her give us the clue to the success of her career.

> *To be deeply in love is, of course, a great liberating force and the most common experience that frees.... Ideally, both members of a couple in love free each other to new and different worlds. I was no exception to the general rule. The sheer fact of finding myself loved was unbelievable and changed my world, my feelings about life and myself. I was given confidence, strength, and almost a new character. The man I was to marry believed in me and what I could do, and consequently I found I could do more than I realized.*

Charles did believe in Anne to an extraordinary degree. He saw beneath her shy surface. He realized that deep down in her innermost well was a wealth of wisdom, a deep, profound, untapped reservoir of ability. Within the security of his love she was freed—*released*—to discover and develop her own capacity, to get in touch with her own feelings, to cultivate her own skills, and to emerge from that cocoon of shyness a beautiful, ever-delicate butterfly whose presence would enhance many lives far beyond the perimeter of her husband's shadow. He encouraged her to do her own kind of flying and he admired her for it.

Does that imply she was a wild, determined, independent wife, bent on "doing her own thing," regardless? Am I leaving that impression? If so, I'm not communicating clearly. Such would be an inaccurate pen portrait of Anne Morrow Lindbergh. She was a butterfly, remember...not a hawk.

Make no mistake about it, this lady was inseparably linked in love to her man. In fact, it was within the comfort of his love that she gleaned the confidence to reach out, far beyond her limited, shy world.

We're talking roots and wings. A husband's love that is strong enough to reassure yet unthreatened enough to release. Tight enough to embrace yet loose enough to enjoy. Magnetic enough to hold, yet magnanimous enough to allow for flight...with an absence of jealousy as others applaud *her* accomplishments and admire *her* competence. Charles, the secure, put away the net so Anne, the shy, could flutter and fly.

THE MISSING CANDELABRA

BRUCE MCIVER
FROM *STORIES I COULDN'T TELL WHILE I WAS A PASTOR*

t was one of the largest weddings ever held at Wilshire. Fifteen minutes before the service was scheduled to begin, the church parking
lots were overflowing with cars and scores of people were crowding into
the foyer, waiting to be properly seated. It was the kind of occasion that
warms the heart of a pastor.

But that was fifteen minutes before the service.

At exactly seven o'clock the mothers were seated, and the organist
sounded the triumphant notes of the processional. That was my cue to
enter the sanctuary through the side door at the front and begin presiding
over the happy occasion. As I reached for the door a voice called from
down the hall, "Not yet, Pastor. Don't open the door. I've got a message
for you."

I turned and through the subdued lighting I saw the assistant florist
hurrying as fast as she could toward me. Her speed didn't set any records
for she was about eight months pregnant and waddled down the hall with
obvious difficulty. She was nearly out of breath when she reached me.
"Pastor," she panted, "we can't find the candelabra that you are supposed
to use at the close of the ceremony. We've looked everywhere, and it just
can't be found. What on earth can we do?"

I sensed immediately that we had a big problem on our hands. The couple to be married had specifically requested that the unity candle be a part of the wedding service. We had gone over it carefully at the rehearsal—step by step. The candelabra, designed to hold three candles, was to be placed near the altar. The mothers of the bride and groom would be ushered down the aisle, each carrying a lighted candle. Upon reaching the front of the sanctuary, they were to move to the candelabra and place their candles in the appropriate receptacles. Throughout the ceremony the mothers' candles were to burn slowly while the larger middle one remained unlighted. After the vows had been spoken, the bride and groom would light the center candle. This was designed to symbolize family unity as well as the light of God's love in the new relationship.

I felt good about all this at the rehearsal. I had a special verse of Scripture that I planned to read as the couple lighted the middle candle. We had it down to perfection.

We thought.

The notes from the organ pealed louder and louder as I was stalled in the hallway. I knew that the organist by now was glancing over her left shoulder wondering where in the world the minister was.

"Okay," I said to the perplexed florist, "we'll just have to 'wing it.' I'll cut that part out of the ceremony and improvise at the close."

With those words I opened the door and entered the sanctuary, muttering behind my frozen smile, "What on earth are we going to do?"

The groom and his attendants followed me in. The bride and her attendants came down the left aisle of the sanctuary. When the first bridesmaid arrived at the front, she whispered something in my direction.

The puzzled look on my face was a signal to her that I did not understand.

She whispered the message again, opening her mouth wider and emphasizing every syllable. By straining to hear above the organ and through lip-reading I made out what she was saying: "Go ahead with the unity candle part of the ceremony."

"But...how?" I whispered through my teeth with a plastic smile.

"Just go ahead," she signaled back.

We made it through the first part of the ceremony without any difficulty.

Everyone was beaming in delight because of the happy occasion—everyone except the first bridesmaid who had brought me the message. When I looked in her direction for some additional word about the candelabra, she had a stoic look on her face and her mouth was tightly clamped shut. Obviously, she was out of messages for me.

We continued with the ceremony. I read a passage from 1 Corinthians 13 and emphasized the importance of love and patience in building a marriage relationship. I asked the bride and groom to join hands, and I began to talk about the vows they would make. There wasn't a hitch. I was beginning to feel better, but I still had to figure out some way to conclude the service. Just now, however, we needed to get through the vows and rings.

"John, in taking the woman whom you hold by your hand to be your wife, do you promise to love her?…"

"That's the funniest thing I've ever seen," the bride interrupted with a loud whisper. I turned from the bewildered groom to look at her and noticed that she was staring toward her right, to the organ side of the front of the sanctuary. Not only was she looking in that direction, so were all the attendants, and so was the audience! One thousand eyes focused on a moving target to my left. I knew it was moving, for heads and eyes followed it, turning ever so slightly in slow motion style.

The moving target was none other than the assistant florist. She had slipped through the door by the organ and was moving on hands and knees behind the choir rail toward the center of the platform where I stood. The dear lady, "great with child," thought she was out of sight, beneath the rail. But in fact, her posterior bobbled in plain view, six inches above the choir rail. As she crawled along she carried in each hand a burning candle. To make matters worse, she didn't realize that she was silhouetted—a large, moving, "pregnant" shadow—on the wall behind the choir loft.

The wedding party experienced the agony of smothered, stifled laughter. Their only release was the flow of hysterical tears while they fought to keep their composure. Two or three of the bride's attendants shook so hard that petals of the flowers in their bouquets fell to the floor.

It was a welcomed moment for me when the vows were completed and I could say with what little piety remained, "Now, let us bow our heads and close our eyes for a special prayer." This was a signal for the soloist to sing "The Lord's Prayer." It also gave me a chance to peep during the singing and to figure out what in the world was happening.

"Pssst! Pssst!"

I did a half turn, looked down, and saw a lighted candle being pushed through the greenery behind me.

"Take this candle," the persistent florist said.

The soloist continued to sing, "Give us this day our daily bread..."

"Pssst. Now take this one," the voice behind me said as a second candle was poked through the greenery.

"...as we forgive those who trespass against us..."

I was beginning to catch on. So I was to be the human candelabra. Here I stood, with a candle in each hand and my Bible and notes tucked under my arm.

"Where's the third candle?" I whispered above the sounds of "...but deliver us from evil..."

"Between my knees," the florist answered. "Just a minute and I'll pass it through to you."

That's when the bride lost it. So did several of the attendants. The last notes of "The Lord's Prayer" were drowned out by the snickers all around me.

I couldn't afford such luxury. Somebody had to carry this thing on to conclusion and try to rescue something from it, candelabra or no candelabra. I determined to do just that as I now tried to juggle three candles, a Bible, and wedding notes. My problem was complicated by the fact that two of the candles were burning, and the third one soon would be.

It was a challenging dilemma, one that called for creative action—in a hurry. And there was nothing in the *Pastor's Manual* that addressed this predicament. Nor had it ever been mentioned in a seminary class on pastoral responsibilities. I was on my own.

I handed one candle to the nearly hysterical bride who was laughing so hard that tears were trickling down her cheeks. I handed the other to the groom who was beginning to question all the reassurances I had passed out freely at the rehearsal. My statements about "no problems," and, "we'll breeze through the service without a hitch," and "just relax and trust me," were beginning to sound hollow.

I held the last candle in my hands. They were to light it together from the ones they were each holding. Miraculously, we made it through that part in spite of jerking hands and tears of smothered laughter. Now we had three burning candles.

In a very soft, reassuring voice, I whispered, "That's fine. Now each of you blow out your candle."

Golly, I said to myself, *we're going to get through this thing yet.*

That thought skipped through my mind just before the bride, still out of control, pulled her candle toward her mouth to blow it out, forgetting that she was wearing a nylon veil over her face.

"Poooff!"

The veil went up in smoke and disintegrated.

Fortunately, except for singed eyebrows, the bride was not injured.

Through the hole in the charred remains of her veil she gave me a bewildered look. I had no more reassurances for her, the groom, or anybody. Enough was enough.

Disregarding my notes concerning the conclusion of the ceremony, I took all the candles and blew them out myself. Then, peering through the smoke of three extinguished candles, I signaled the organist to begin the recessional…now! Just get us out of here! Quickly!

Everything else is a blur.

But I still turn pale when prospective brides tell me about "this wonderful idea of using a unity candle" in the ceremony.

LIFE LESSONS FROM LOVEBIRDS

VICKIE LYNNE AGEE

ecently, my husband and I were walking through a local mall near closing time, when we decided to stop and take a look around the pet store. As we made our way past the cages of poodles and Pomeranians, tabby cats and turtles, our eyes caught sight of something that immediately charmed us: a pair of peach-faced lovebirds. Unlike many other lovebirds we encountered there, this particular pair looked truly "in love." In fact, they snuggled and cuddled next to each other the whole time we watched them. Throughout the next few days, my mind returned to the image of those two delightful birds. I admired their devotion, and felt their very presence inspiring.

Apparently, these birds had the same effect on my husband, because he showed up late from work one night shortly thereafter, clutching an elegant birdcage that housed those two precious creatures, and introduced them as new additions to the family. For days we wrestled with names of well-known couples, coming up with everything from Ricky and Lucy and George and Gracie to Wilma and Fred. But finally we decided on Ozzie and Harriet—a gentle reminder of a simpler day when love and togetherness between couples were not only a commitment, but a way of life.

And so it is with this in mind that I have watched these lovebirds and made the following observations about life and love.

1. If you spend too much time looking in the mirror, it's easy to lose your balance.
2. Always keep a pleasant look on your face, even if your cage needs cleaning.
3. If your mate wants to share your perch with you, move over.
4. The real treats in life usually come only after you've cracked a few hulls.
5. It takes two to snuggle.
6. Sometimes your mate can see mites you didn't even know you had.
7. Singing draws more affection than squawking.
8. It is only when your feathers get ruffled that your true colors really show.
9. Too many toys can be distracting.
10. When you have love in your heart, everyone around you will find joy in your presence.

WISE MOTHER

A mother who had a rather large number of children was being interviewed by a newspaper reporter. He asked, "Which one of your children do you love the most?" Her reply indicated what a wise and loving mother she was: "I love the one most who is away from home until he returns; the one who is sick until he is well; the one who is hurt until the hurt disappears; and the one who is lost until he is found."

AUTHOR UNKNOWN

HEROES AND HEROINES

WILLIAM E. BARTON
FROM *PARABLES OF A COUNTRY PARSON*
"UNUSAL TYPESETTING PERSERVED FROM ORIGINAL TEXT."

There came to me a man and a woman, even an Husband and his Wedded Wife and they said, We are weary one of the other.

And I said, Why is it thus?

And they said, We have grown commonplace to each other. Once we were to each other an Hero and an Heroine, but now we are Neither.

And I said, Napoleon did not look heroic to Josephine after she had seen him with his Suspenders hanging down his back; neither did Joan of Arc look heroic when she held her Front Hair in her mouth while she did up her back hair.

And they said, But he was an Hero and she was an Heroine.

And I said, Heroes and Heroines cannot appear heroic all the time. Caesar did not look heroic when he had pushed his slippers too far back under the bed, and he had to get down and fish them out with an umbrella; but that be a necessary thing, even to Heroes and Heroines.

And I said to the woman, When the Baby was sick, eight years ago, did not this thine Husband watch with thee day and night?

And she said, He did.

And I said unto the man, When thou hadst lost half thy money in a

Fool Speculation, did she not stick by thee like a Little Burr, and cheer thee up, and never say, I told thee so?

And he said, It is even so.

And I said, Go down on your knees.

And they knelt.

And I said, Join hands.

And they did so.

And I prayed to God on their behalf, till there came to their eyes tears of Memory and Love.

And I smote them, lightly on the back, and I said, I dub thee an Hero; I dub thee an Heroine.

And I sent them forth.

And they lived happily ever afterward.

HEART OF THE MATTER

Teaching creative writing to an elementry-school class, I closed with a question: "How do you know your grandmother loves you?" A little boy waved his hand with enthusiasm. When I called on him, he said, "I know my grandma loves me 'cause when I look in her eyes, I can see all the way to her heart."

AUTHOR UNKNOWN
FROM *GRANDPARENTING BY GRACE*

THE OTHER WOMAN

DAVID FARRELL

*A*fter 21 years of marriage, I've discovered a new way of keeping the spark of love and intimacy alive in my relationship with my wife:

I've recently started dating another woman.

It was my wife's idea, actually. "You know you love her," she said one day, taking me by surprise. "Life is too short. You need to spend time with the people you love."

"But I love *you*," I protested.

"I know. But you also love her. You probably won't believe me, but I think that if the two of you spend more time together, it will bring the two of us closer."

As usual, Peggy was right.

The other woman that my wife was encouraging me to date was my mother.

My mom is a seventy-one-year-old widow who has lived alone since my father died nineteen years ago. Right after his death, I moved 2,500 miles away to California, where I started my own family and career. When I moved back near my hometown five years ago, I promised myself I would spend more time with her. But somehow with the demands of my job and three kids, I never got around to seeing her much beyond family get-togethers and holidays.

She was surprised and suspicious when I called and suggested the two of us go out to dinner and a movie. "What's wrong? Are you moving my grandchildren away?" she asked. My mother is the type of woman who thinks anything out of the ordinary—a late-night phone call or a surprise dinner invitation from her eldest son—signals bad news.

"I thought it would be nice to spend some time with you," I said. "Just the two of us."

She considered that statement for a moment.

"I'd like that," she said. "I'd like that a lot."

I found myself nervous as I drove to her house Friday after work. I had the predate jitters—and all I was doing was going out with my mother, for Pete's sake!

What would we talk about? What if she didn't like the restaurant I chose? Or the movie?

What if she didn't like either?

When I pulled into her driveway, I realized how excited she, too, was about our date. She was waiting by the door with her coat on. Her hair was curled. She was smiling. "I told my lady friends that I was going out with my son, and they were all impressed," she said as she got into my car. "They can't wait until tomorrow to hear about our evening."

We didn't go anywhere fancy, just a neighborhood place where we could talk. When we got there my mother clutched my arm—half out of affection and half to help her negotiate the steps into the dining room.

Once we were seated, I had to read the menu for both of us. Her eyes only see large shapes and shadows. Halfway through listing the entrées, I glanced up. Mom was sitting across the table, just looking at me. A wistful smile traced her lips.

"I used to be the menu reader when you were little," she said.

I understood instantly what she was saying. From caregiver to cared-for, from cared-for to caregiver; our relationship had come full circle.

"Then it's time for you to relax and let me return the favor," I said.

We had a nice talk over dinner. Nothing earth-shattering, just catching up with each other's lives. We talked so much that we missed the movie. "I'll go out with you again, but only if you let me buy dinner next time," my mother said as I dropped her off. I agreed.

"How was your date?" my wife wanted to know when I got home that night.

"Nice…nicer than I thought it would be," I said.

She smiled her I-told-you-so smile.

Since that night I've been dating Mom regularly. We don't go out every week, but we try to see each other at least a couple of times a month. We always have dinner, and sometimes we take in a movie, too. Mostly, though, we just talk. I tell her about my daily trials at work. I brag about the kids and my wife. She fills me in on the family gossip I can never seem to keep up on.

She also tells me about her past. Now I know what it was like for my mom to work in a factory during World War II. I know about how she met my father there, and how they nurtured a trolley-car courtship through those difficult times. As I've listened to these stories, I've come to realize how important they are to me. They are my history. I can't get enough of them.

But we don't just talk about the past. We also talk about the future. Because of health problems, my mother worries about the days ahead. "I have so much living to do," she told me one night. "I need to be there while my grandchildren grow up. I don't want to miss *any* of it."

Like a lot of my baby-boomer friends, I tend to rush around, filling my At-a-Glance calendar to the brim as I struggle to fit a career, family and relationships into my life. I often complain about how quickly time flies. Spending time with my mom has taught me the importance of slowing down. I finally understand the meaning of a term I've heard a million times: quality time.

Peggy was right. Dating another woman *has* helped my marriage. It has made me a better husband and father, and hopefully, a better son.

Thanks, Mom. I love you.

CIRCLE OF LOVE

JEANNIE S. WILLIAMS

When Joey was five years old his kindergarten teacher told the class to draw a picture of something they loved. Joey drew a picture of his family…and then he took his red crayon and drew a big circle around the stick figures on his paper. Joey wanted to write a word at the top of the circle so he got up from his chair and approached the teacher's desk.

"Teacher," he asked, "How do you spell…?"

But before he could finish his question the teacher told him to go back to his seat and not interrupt the class again. Joey folded the paper and stuck it in his pocket.

When Joey got home from school that day, he remembered his drawing and dug it out of his pocket. He smoothed it out on the kitchen table, got a pencil from his backpack, and looked at the big red circle. Joey's mother was busy cooking supper but Joey wanted to finish the picture before he showed it to her…

"Mom, how do you spell…?"

"Joey, can't you see I'm busy right now? Why don't you go outside and play…and don't slam the door," she told him.

Joey folded the drawing and stuck it back in his pocket. Later that evening, Joey dug the picture out of his pocket again. He looked at the big red circle and then ran into the kitchen to get a pencil. He wanted to finish his drawing before he showed it to his father. Joey smoothed out all the wrinkles and laid the picture on the floor near his dad's big recliner.

"Daddy, how do you spell…?"

"Joey, I'm reading the paper right now and I don't want to be bothered. Why don't you go outside and play…and don't slam the door."

Joey folded the drawing and put it in his pocket. His mom found the drawing the next morning while she was doing the laundry. She threw it in the trash without ever opening it, along with a small rock, a piece of string, and two marbles Joey had found while he was outside playing.

When Joe was twenty-eight years old, his daughter Annie drew a picture. It was a picture of their family. Joe laughed when five-year-old Annie pointed to a squiggle stick figure and said, "That's you, Daddy!"

Annie laughed, too. Joe looked at the big red circle his daughter had drawn around the stick figures and he began to slowly trace the circle with his finger.

"I'll be right back," Annie said as she jumped off her father's lap. When she came back she had a pencil clutched in her small hand. Her father moved the drawing aside to make room on his lap for his small daughter.

Annie positioned the pencil point near the top of the big red circle. "Daddy, how do you spell love?" she asked.

Joe gathered the child in his arms and guided her small hand as he helped her form the letters.

"Love is spelled T-I-M-E," he told her.

JUST ONE KISS!

ANN PLATZ AND SUSAN WALES
FROM *A MATCH MADE IN HEAVEN*

M r. Baumann's doctors had warned him and his wife that he was at high risk for a heart attack. But when the attack actually came, Mrs. Baumann still wasn't prepared. Gripped with shock, fear, and panic, she rode by her husband's side in the ambulance, repeatedly crying out to God to save him.

At the hospital, the nurses had to pull Mrs. Baumann away from her husband so the doctors could examine him. After they had successfully stabilized his heart, Mrs. Baumann rushed down the hall to the telephones to call each of their seven children. With tears of exhaustion and relief, she told them of their father's heart attack, assuring them that his condition was now stable.

But when Mrs. Baumann returned to her husband's room, she gasped at the sight before her. Two nurses stood over her husband. Tubes ran in and out of his trembling body, and machines and monitors were humming and beeping. His face was bright red, and he was gasping for breath.

"What have you done to my husband?" she cried.

One of the nurses explained, as sympathetically as possible, that he had suffered a massive stroke.

A stroke! On top of the heart attack! Mrs. Baumann couldn't control her emotions. Overcome with grief and blinded by tears, she grabbed her husband's head off the pillow. She held him tightly in her arms, calling out his name and kissing his lips.

At that very moment, the doctor walked in and demanded, "Mrs. Baumann, what do you think you're doing?"

She turned to the doctor and hotly declared, "The question is, Doctor, what have you done to my husband?"

The doctor shook his head and chuckled, "Mrs. Baumann. That is not your husband!"

For a moment, Mrs. Baumann was so stunned she couldn't speak. Then she looked more carefully at the man on the bed.

"He's...he's...not!" she cried, turning a dark shade of crimson. "Oh no! Oh dear! Oh no!"

Gently a nurse escorted the mortified Mrs. Baumann out into the hall.

"Why didn't that man try to stop me?" asked Mrs. Baumann.

"Because of his stroke, he's unable to move or to speak," the nurse answered.

Mrs. Baumann gasped. "And now he must be wondering why that strange lady kissed him!"

As soon as they entered her husband's room, Mrs. Baumann rushed to her husband's side and kissed him. Then, still very shaken, she related her mistake. "He had so many tubes and...and...I hope I didn't hurt him, Bernie!"

Mr. Baumann smiled and assured his wife that the man was probably feeling better than ever. But Mrs. Baumann decided she better go down to the chapel to pray for both Bernie and the man she'd kissed—and perhaps made worse!

A few days later the doctor dropped by Mr. Baumann's room for his final checkup. "Mrs. Baumann," he said, "You'll be glad to know that your husband and my patient across the hall have both made miraculous recoveries. Do you suppose it was my good doctoring, your prayers, or your passionate kisses?"

"Why, why..." she fumbled.

"Maybe it was all three!" the doctor added with a wink.

I LOVED YOU
ENOUGH TO...

ERMA BOMBECK
FROM *FOREVER, ERMA*

ou don't love me!"

How many times have your kids laid that one on you? And how many times have you, as a parent, resisted the urge to tell them how much?

Someday, when my children are old enough to understand the logic that motivates a mother, I'll tell them:

> I loved you enough to bug you about where you were going, with whom and what time you would get home.
>
> I loved you enough to insist you buy a bike with your own money even though we could afford it.
>
> I loved you enough to be silent and let you discover your friend was a creep.
>
> I loved you enough to make you return a Milky Way with a bite out of it to the drugstore and confess, "I stole this."
>
> I loved you enough to stand over you for two hours while you cleaned your bedroom, a job that would have taken me 15 minutes.

I loved you enough to say, "Yes, you can go to Disney World on Mother's Day."

I loved you enough to let you see anger, disappointment, disgust and tears in my eyes.

I loved you enough not to make excuses for your lack of respect or your bad manners.

I loved you enough to admit that I was wrong and ask for your forgiveness.

I loved you enough to ignore what every other mother did or said.

I loved you enough to let you stumble, fall, hurt and fail.

I loved you enough to let you assume the responsibility for your own actions at age 6, 10 or 16.

I loved you enough to figure you would lie about the party being chaperoned but forgave you for it—after discovering I was right.

I loved you enough to accept you for what you are, not what I wanted you to be.

But, most of all, I loved you enough to say no when you hated me for it. That was the hardest part of all.

My Daughter-in-Law

There are no words that I am master of
With which to thank you, God, for my son's wife—
This girl who is part mother in her love,
Part young girl, and part woman, and her life
So gathered up in flame to meet the one
Who is my son.

I yield him to her, I who have so long
Been lovingly preparing him for her.
I would not bind them with one selfish thong
That through its constant chafing might deter
Their love upon the high road, they must be
Free as the wind is free.
Dear God, I am so grateful that my son
In searching for a woman found this one.

AUTHOR UNKNOWN

Encouragement

THE PROGNOSIS

A young mother who had been diagnosed with a treatable form of cancer returned home from the hospital self-conscious about her physical appearance and loss of hair following radiation. Upon sitting down on a kitchen chair, her son appeared quietly in the doorway studying her curiously. As his mother began a rehearsed speech to help him understand what he was seeing, the boy came forward to snuggle in her lap. Intently, he laid his head to her chest and just held on. As his mother was saying, "And sometime, hopefully soon, I will look the way I used to, and then I'll be better," the boy sat up thoughtfully. With six-year-old frankness he simply responded, "Different hair. Same old heart."

His mother no longer had to wait for "sometime, hopefully soon" to be better. She was.

ROCHELLE M. PENNINGTON

THE SPIRIT OF HOSPITALITY

EMILIE BARNES
FROM *THE SPIRIT OF LOVELINESS*

The "parlor" was tiny, just an extra room behind the store. But the tablecloth was spotless, the candles were glowing, the flowers were bright, the tea was fragrant. Most of all, the smile was genuine and welcoming whenever my mother invited people to "come on back for a cup of tea."

How often I heard her say those words when I was growing up. And how little I realized the mark they would make on me.

Those were hard years after my father died, when Mama and I shared three rooms behind her little dress shop. Mama waited on the customers, did alterations, and worked on the books until late at night. I kept house—planning and shopping for meals, cooking, cleaning, doing laundry—while going to school and learning the dress business as well.

Sometimes I felt like Cinderella—work, work, work. And the little girl in me longed for a Prince Charming to carry me away to his castle. There I would preside over a grand and immaculate household, waited on hand and foot by attentive servants. I would wear gorgeous dresses and entertain kings and queens who marveled at my beauty and my wisdom and brought me lavish gifts.

But in the meantime, of course, I had work to do. And although I didn't know it, I was already receiving a gift more precious than any dream castle could be. For unlike Cinderella, I lived with a loving Mama who understood the true meaning of sharing and joy—a Mama who brightened people's lives with the spirit of hospitality.

Our customers quickly learned that Mama offered a sympathetic ear as well as elegant clothes and impeccable service. Often they ended up sharing their hurts and problems with her. And then, inevitably, would come the invitation: "Let me make you a cup of tea." She would usher our guests back to our main room, which served as a living room by day and a bedroom by night. Quickly a fresh cloth was slipped on the table, a candle lit, fresh flowers set out if possible, and the teapot heated. If we had them, she would pull out cookies or a loaf of banana bread. There was never anything fancy, but the gift of her caring warmed many a heart on a cold night.

My Mama's willingness to open her life to others—to share her home, her food, and her love—was truly a royal gift. She passed it along to me, and I have the privilege of passing it on to others. What a joy to be part of the spirit of hospitality!

Treat people as if they were what they ought to be and you help them become what they are capable of being.

GOETHE

GRADUATING WITH HONOR

JEAN MARIE LASKAS
FROM *THE WASHINGTON POST MAGAZINE*

I met Eileen, my brother John's wife, when I was seven. Only she wasn't his wife then. She was an amazing 19-year-old with blond streaks in her hair who was exotic and funny and terrified of my parents. The first time she came for dinner, I loved her immediately.

This was back in the days of formal meals. Eileen dropped two peas in her lap, then two more and then another. She thought nobody saw. After dinner I told her, "I saw the peas, but I won't tell." Thirty-one years have passed, and this is the first time I've said anything.

It's okay—she said I could. We were talking on the phone, right around her 50th birthday. She was describing what 50 felt like. Brainwise, she said, she'd sometimes felt my sisters and I had passed her long ago. There were times she felt left out.

For my sisters and me, the natural order of things was high school, college. But Eileen worked while John went through medical school. She went to college afterward but dropped out her junior year. By then she had babies, and she chose to be a full-time mother. You never saw a happier mom.

"And you never knew how I ached," she said. She told me about the college ring she got before she dropped out. She wore it for years but decided one day to take it off. "A woman recognized it and asked when I graduated," Eileen explained. "I said, 'Actually I didn't.' She said, 'Then why are you wearing the ring?' I thought, *She's right. I am pretending to be someone I'm not.*"

Then just a few years ago Eileen started talking about going back to school. She didn't make a big deal out of it. I didn't think it was one.

Now I understand. An unfulfilled promise to yourself can seem so tiny to everyone else as to be imperceptible. But so can a grain of sand in your eye.

So Eileen signed up for two courses at the college she had left 18 years before. The first day of class she put the ring back on. She got books, test dates, assignments. She thought, *There is no way I can do this.*

She got an A and a B+.

The following semester she signed up for five courses and committed herself to write a senior thesis on Charles Dickens. She aced them all. Last spring she graduated. She said she hadn't been this happy since she was 19.

The happiness, she explained, was only incidentally about a college degree. She told me about her sons Joe and John cooking dinner while she was off at class. About her daughter, Alyson, cleaning the house so Mom could study. About her husband, John, tutoring her in chemistry. She told me who proofread her thesis: her youngest son, Tom, then in eighth grade.

Because of her family, not despite it, she made it. And this circle of give and take and give has made 50 the greatest age to be.

(Reprinted with permission from the April 1997 *Reader's Digest*)

THE POINSETTIAS

LOUISE CARROLL
FROM *THE LUTHERAN DIGEST*

There were many poinsettia plants in church this year, and they were particularly full and deep red. As our Sunday school class was meeting before church, the topic of discussion was about these plants.

"Aren't they beautiful!" "This is the prettiest I've ever seen them." And then the question, "Why do we have poinsettias at Christmas?"

Millie said, "Because they look so nice." Anne said, "Because they look like Christmas—all red and green." Bill ventured, "Maybe some ancient superstition that has been forgotten." But most of the answers were, "I don't know." However, Aunt Jennie, who is wiser than the rest of us, said, "So God can use them to a good purpose."

At the Christmas Eve service, the poinsettias were placed across the front, on the lectern and on the windowsills. Certainly it seemed they had been put there to add beauty.

On Christmas morning, the poinsettias looked even more beautiful. Pastor McNulty announced to the congregation that those who had purchased the poinsettias should be sure to take them home after the service. But how was that he said it? "It would be a help to the ladies who are taking care of the plants if you would take your poinsettia home after the service."

Seven-year-old Bettie poked her sister, Bonnie, in the ribs and whispered excitedly, "Did you hear that? Did you? Did you? Now we have a Christmas gift for Mommy."

"Wow, Bettie, I prayed we would have a gift for Mommy."

Only a look from the kindly but stern-looking Miss Nelson quieted the two little girls.

After the service, my friend, Ethel, was in charge of putting the poinsettias in plastic sleeves to protect them from the cold, bitter wind. As the crowd thinned out, two little girls approached Ethel. Ethel recognized Bettie and Bonnie as the daughters of Judy, a single parent who was going to school and working. Judy never came to church but she brought Bettie and Bonnie.

Bonnie, by virtue of being the oldest at eight years, spoke with assurance to Ethel, "We are going to give our poinsettia to our mother for Christmas."

It was a small church and Ethel was in charge of the poinsettias and so, although she kept careful notes, she was aware in her mind that neither Judy nor her children had purchased a poinsettia.

Ethel smiled and said, "I know your mother is going to be thrilled with such a nice gift."

Picking the fullest, reddest poinsettia she could find, Ethel lovingly slipped the plastic sleeve on it and handed it to Bonnie. Almost bouncing with excitement, the two little girls hurried out the door.

After everyone had left and Ethel was alone, she sat in the front pew a few minutes to think. There were still a few poinsettias left and on Monday she would deliver them to the nursing home.

How interesting, Ethel thought, *Pastor McNulty hadn't made it clear about the poinsettias. It sounded as though there was one for everyone who wanted it.*

Ethel smiled. Why do we put poinsettias in the church at Christmas? Just like Aunt Jennie said, "So God can use them for a good purpose."

A TIME TO SCATTER

MARY PIELENZ HAMPTON
FROM *A TEA FOR ALL SEASONS*

One afternoon when I was about 18 years old, I left our house and walked the four blocks to the downtown area, hoping to find someone or something to lift my spirits.

I found a friend working at a shop, and her day was even worse than mine. As I walked on though, I passed an open-air flower stand with some of the season's first daffodils. Their cheerful sunniness stood out in dramatic contrast to the drippy gray of the streets and the skies. I purchased a half dozen, knowing that they would brighten my room at home.

On the way home, I stopped and gave a couple of them to my friend, hoping to cheer her up. A little bit further along my route, I encountered a lighthearted street person who commented on the flowers. I gave him one too.

At the last corner before my house, there was a shop that I passed nearly every day on my way to and from church and school. My path often crossed with a man who worked there—his big, booming voice a disconcerting contrast to the disabled body in his wheelchair. His greeting was always warm and friendly, but I was intimidated and usually kept my response brief as I hurried on my way.

On this day, my feet took over and I walked past the crosswalk and into the store before my mind had a chance to stop them. I walked up to the counter, and thrust the three remaining daffodils toward him saying, "These are for you, because daffodils are cheerful and you're always cheerful." Still in disbelief at what I had done, I turned and left before he had an opportunity to respond.

I walked home the remaining block a different person. Even though I went without the flowers that I had purchased to cheer myself, the sunshine that came from my heart illuminated my path as though the sun itself had broken through the clouds. The simple act of giving away something that I wanted changed me. I was no longer intimidated by the man at the shop in the corner. I had seen a glimmer that I could be a giving person.

Plant a word of love heart-deep in a person's life.
Nurture it with a smile and a prayer and watch what happens.

MAX LUCADO

P.S. I LOVE YOU

H. JACKSON BROWN, JR.
FROM *P.S. I LOVE YOU*

Over the years Mom has written my sister and me hundreds of letters. What was cherished most were the little P.S. notes she would write at the end of each one. There, in just a few words, she would encourage and inspire us with keen observations, gentle humor, and loving advice.

This is a sampling of her P.S. messages we love the most. Although some were written more than forty years ago, they still ring with truth and insight.

> *P.S. Regarding your D in biology, let me only say that sometimes a scare is worth more than good advice.*
> I love you,
> Mom

> *P.S. Uncle Henry says he knows he's getting old because last week thieves broke into his car and stole his cassette deck, but left his tapes.*
> I love you,
> Mom

P.S. The great man shows his greatness by the way he treats the little man.

> *I love you,*
> *Mom*

P.S. Someone asked me last week what I did. I thought for a moment and answered, "Explorer." I was pleased with my reply.

> *I love you,*
> *Mom*

P.S. Your father defines an honest man as someone you could play checkers with over the telephone.

> *I love you,*
> *Mom*

P.S. Your father says inflation hasn't ruined everything. A dime can still be used as a screwdriver.

> *I love you,*
> *Mom*

P.S. I saw a sign with the word FIDO on the back of a Winnebago at a filling station. I asked the driver if it was the name of his dog. "Oh no," he replied. "It's to remind me that when someone is discourteous on the road I should just "Forget It and Drive On." Good advice.

> *I love you,*
> *Mom*

P.S. Be smarter than other people—just don't tell them so.

> *I love you,*
> *Mom*

P.S. When you have nothing important or interesting to say, don't let anyone persuade you to say it.

     I love you,
     Mom

P.S. Remember the Golden Rule. And remember it's your turn.

     I love you,
     Mom

My sister and I can't wait until the next letter arrives.

THANKS FOR THE MIRACLE, SIS

JANN MITCHELL
FROM *THE OREGONIAN* NEWSPAPER

My Dear Sister Sally,

This is a thank-you letter, shared in public because—as you say—it may hold hope to others.

When I left you in the rehab center in mid-November, a week and a half after your second stroke, at age 46, you were paralyzed on your left side, confined to bed, confused about what was happening. Doctors said you could die, or at best subsist with extensive brain damage.

Thank you for proving them wrong.

Oh, the joy of having you and our younger sister, Jill, meet me at the airport in mid-January, just two months later! Precious, upright you—leaning on your cane, your hair freshly cut and styled, and tears running down your face. Were your cheeks wetter than mine?

We came to make sure that you would be safe at home alone until your son got home from school and your husband home from work. Those few days showed us you would, and taught me far more than I can tell you.

Sure, you still have weakness in your left arm and a slight hearing loss. You mispronounce some words and get confused if we talk too fast, but you are intact: your keen intelligence, your delicious sense of humor, your thoughtfulness and generosity, your sweet soul. More folks should be as whole as you are.

And now we see a new side to the shy and sometimes fearful middle sister who preferred to stick close to home, while Jill and I ventured forth and got into trouble. Thank you for your example in courage, fortitude and the ability to keep putting one foot in front of the other in the face of great odds.

I watched you exercising several times daily to strengthen your left arm: stacking dice and paper cups, moving a dish towel around the table in figure-eights, laboriously picking up paper clips and small screws to drop into a cup.

I saw you punch numbers into the automatic teller machine to get your bank balance, then do it all again when you forgot the sum. And I was suddenly ashamed that some days simply getting out of bed seems like too much work.

Thank you for the laughter. When you go to have your blood checked weekly to make sure your blood thinner's working, you say you have an appointment at "the vampire's." When you looked at the bleak hospital photos I'd snapped of you attached to snakelike tubes, you said, "I was really having a bad hair day!" Boy, are you a lesson in lightening up.

Stopping by your office gave us the opportunity to see how much others care about you (something some folks never discover until a funeral). Your co-workers told me how helpful you'd been when their relatives suffered strokes. They talked about your enthusiasm and generosity when they had babies, or adopted a family at Christmas. Such an outpouring of love!

Several times you apologized for "being trouble." Don't you know how grateful we are, dear Sally, to finally be able to give back to you? Who else but you would present Christmas gifts in January—gifts you'd purchased long before the stroke, now wrapped in paper bags with bows because you couldn't manage gift-wrapping?

Thank you for pointing out what's truly important—and for saying that you've dropped from your list nagging your teenager about his room. "I used to worry about things I thought were problems—like being fat," you said. "Fat isn't a problem. Being healthy is the most important thing in the world." Let me remember that the next time I climb on the scale.

And thanks, too, for the lesson in gentleness with yourself. When you pulled your shirt on inside-out and we called it to your attention, you didn't beat yourself up for making a mistake as the rest of us do so often when we don't do something perfectly. You simply said, "Oops, I flunked shirt!" and fixed it.

I'm the wordsmith, but you say things better. Like when you read through all the nice letters that readers sent when I wrote about your stroke. "People are really nice, aren't they?" you said through tears. And over cocoa, you remarked, "I'm so glad I didn't die. I woulda' missed you guys."

We would have missed you, too, Sal. But I want you to know: As painful and as frustrating as this whole experience has been for you and everyone who cares about you, it has been rich in love and lessons. I'm thankful for that.

Because of you, I'll be more patient with the person walking slowly in front of me, or trying to figure out change. Who knows what odds they contend with, that stranger who is someone's father or mother or sister.

And I'm glad you're mine. My miracle sister.

I love you,

Janny

HI, I'M JOEY!

EVELYN PETTY

Believe it or not, I was looking forward to eleven hours on an airplane. There were two reasons. First and foremost I was on my way to London to see our daughter and son-in-law; it had been nine months since our last visit and I missed them fiercely. Second, I was physically and mentally exhausted. The five hours to D.C., then another six to Heathrow, seemed barely enough to rest from my usually frenetic schedule. I hoped to sleep for most of the flight, and John Grisham's latest novel lay inside the very top of my carry-on, waiting to captivate my few waking hours.

As I bumped my way down the aisle, my seat found me before I realized I was even getting close. A bright-eyed little boy greeted me with a big grin. "Hi, I'm Joey! I bet this is where you sit!" he said as he bounded across from the aisle seat to the window. In my sweetest voice I quickly said, "No, I don't think…" but a glance at my boarding pass showed he was right. Well then, surely his mother is the lady across the aisle from us. *I'll simply trade seats,* I thought.

Within moments I felt my trip had taken a serious downward turn. Joey was not only flying alone but he had not stopped to take a breath since his initial greeting. Smiley, blond, blue-eyed, cute—but still a six-year-old boy. As the stewardess gave me a wink, I began to feel "had." Longing for the restful flight I had anticipated, I tried to ignore Joey but his constant chatter was one question after another in an attempt to engage me in conversation. It worked.

As the plane backed out of the gate, I asked him where he was going. The big beaming smile now turned serious as he told me he was going home to Richmond, Virginia, where he lived with his dad. "I've been in Portland seeing my mom for two weeks." There was a long pause and then, "I really want to live with her," as tears started to fall from his cheeks. "I really love my mom and I didn't want to leave."

As the plane lifted into the air, my only thought was whether five hours was long enough to mend the heart of a little boy "barely six years old."

I don't remember all that I said but soon he was off on several other subjects, the smile was back, and we were coloring, reading, playing with anything and everything. As we ate French toast and sausage with lots of syrup, Joey talked about whatever popped into his head. Quite innocently he said, "I like beer. My mom and her boyfriend let me try some beer." I proceeded to give Joey a firm, no-nonsense lecture on why he should not taste beer or anything with alcohol in it, all the while thinking, *What kind of life is this for one so young?*

About four hours into our flight Joey started to get sleepy. Soon his head was on my lap, his little shoes on the floor beside me, and he was fast asleep. I choked back tears as I began to pray for him. Joey had found his way into my heart.

After some time I realized the stewardess in the aisle beside me was bending down with two snack boxes and a look that said she wanted to talk. She thanked me very much for all I had done to care for Joey, then dropping her voice said she had been the one to check him as he boarded the plane in Portland. "His mom just threw the papers at me and took off with about three guys. She didn't even kiss Joey good-bye!"

The true picture of Joey's mom was beginning to come together. What other dreams were going on in this little blond head, dreams that tried to make real life a little more bearable?

Just then the pilot made the announcement to fasten our seat belts in preparation for landing. I quickly grabbed the two miniature Butterfinger bars out of the boxes, and the stewardess left to pick up the last few things from other passengers. I wiggled the seat belt around Joey and as the wheels hit the runway, his eyes popped wide open.

"We're in Washington, D.C., where your father is going to meet you, Joey. I have something for you," I said, and pulled out the two candy bars. "One for you and one for your dad." He jumped straight up and into my arms, giving me a big hug. "You are the nicest lady I have ever met," he exclaimed. "I will never forget you as long as I live."

Nor I you, I thought, smiling over his shoulder and blinking away sudden hot tears. *I'll pray for you, Joey, whenever I see a little boy alone on an airplane. Whenever I see a Butterfinger candy bar. Whenever I read about children paying the price for wayward parents.* As I connected with my next flight, I felt sadness for this child, but also gratitude that God had given me the privilege of caring for one so needy of love and attention. Joey is truly mine for life.

A smile of encouragement at the right moment may act like sunlight on a closed-up flower; it may be the turning point for a struggling life.

AUTHOR UNKNOWN

WITH A CHILD'S HELP

LIZ CURTIS HIGGS
FROM *ONLY ANGELS CAN WING IT*

*K*aryn from Missouri was intent on helping her sons develop positive self-esteem. When she would hear them belittling themselves ("I'm so stupid," "I'm ugly," "I can't do anything right") she would give them a special hand signal, and they begrudgingly changed their tune to "I'm very smart, I'm talented, I can do anything I put my mind to, and I love myself." One morning when she was getting ready for a community conference that she was in charge of, she was mentally reviewing the day's activities.

"A thought began to gnaw at me: 'Does the meeting start at 9:30 or 8:30?' Surely, I would have remembered. Still, the doubts hung on. I climbed from the shower and phoned my co-coordinator. Her husband answered, 'Cyndi's long gone. The conference started an hour ago.' My worst fears snapped to reality. How could I have committed such an oversight? I screamed at my children, 'Throw on your clothes—quick! We gotta go, *now*!'

"Splashing on my make-up, I was muttering aloud, 'I'm such an idiot. I don't deserve to be in charge. What a dumb thing to do...' While I rambled on, verbally kicking myself, my youngest son walked up, put his hands gently around my face, locked his gaze with mine and said, 'You're beautiful, you're smart, you're talented, you can do anything you put your mind to, and *we love you!*'"

LIKE LIGHT SWITCHES

Affirming words from moms and dads are like light switches. Speak a word of affirmation at the right moment in a child's life and it's like lighting up a whole roomful of possibilities.

GARY SMALLEY AND JOHN TRENT
FROM *LEAVING THE LIGHT ON*

IT'S NOT MY SPORT

BETTY J. JOHNSON

*H*ey, guys. Up and at 'em. Today is the day we sign you all up for baseball," a young mother called to her triplet sons.

Three sleepy six-year-old brothers trudged down the steps, crawled up on their stools, perched their elbows on the breakfast bar, chins resting in hands, and said, "Can we have some cereal...please?"

After munching for five minutes, Riley, the fairest of the boys, whined, "Mom, do I have to play? You know, baseball is not my sport. I play soccer and hockey," he added.

Knowing Riley's tendency toward bashfulness and his ongoing anxiety about attempting new things, his mother suggested, "How about trying it for one year with Nate and Kit, please. Then, if it's still not 'your sport,' I won't sign you up next year. Okay?"

"Okay," Riley muttered.

Three weeks later, on the day of the first game, Riley grumbled all the way to the ball field. "I told you this is not my sport, Mom," he hedged. "I wish you hadn't signed me up."

The first inning found the pint-sized towhead in an oversized yellow shirt shuffling around near first base. Suddenly, the first batter hit a grounder toward Riley. He reached down, scooped up the ball, and ran to the bag. The next batter dribbled a hit to the pitcher who slung it in Riley's direction. Riley stuck out his glove, caught the ball, and tagged the base.

He briefly turned toward the bleachers, peeked at his mother, tipped up the bill of his man-sized cap, broke into a wide toothless grin, and raised his thumb.

On the way home, three excited boys filled the car with laughter and chatter. However, as they neared their house, Riley nestled in the front seat, leaned toward his mother and quietly said, "Hey, Mom, I'll bet you didn't know I could play first base so good, did you?"

"Well, Riley, I thought you could play, but no, I didn't know you could play so good," she answered.

"Me neither, Mom," Riley whispered. "Me neither."

What sunshine is to flowers, smiles are to humanity.
They are but trifles, to be sure but, scattered along life's pathway,
the good they do is inconceivable.

JOSEPH ADDISON

THE MOST BEAUTIFUL CAKE

ELLEN JAVERNICK
FROM *THE CHRISTIAN READER*

It was the most beautiful cake in the world. I was seven then, but I still remember it well. Mother and I baked it together. I got to break the eggs and measure the sugar. I greased the pans carefully so the cakes wouldn't stick. We stirred the batter hard. We didn't want the cakes to be lumpy. Then Mother put the pans in the oven to bake. I set the timer. Mother went upstairs to fold clothes, while I sat at the kitchen table and made Daddy's birthday card. The cake was for him and it was going to be perfect.

The timer hadn't rung yet, but I couldn't wait any longer. I opened the oven for just one peek. The cakes were beautiful—rounded on the top and golden brown on the edges. Just then I heard Mother coming down the stairs. I felt a bit guilty about peeking so I quickly slammed the oven door. The slam came at just the wrong time. The still soft centers of both layers collapsed. When Mom opened the oven door a few minutes later, our beautiful cakes looked like soup bowls.

I cried uncontrollably. Our wonderful surprise was ruined!

"Well, let's see," said Mother, matter of factly, over my sobs. "What can we do about these funny looking cakes?" She began by making the frosting. "White will look nice," she commented. I watched as she turned out the layers onto the cooling racks. "Look how perfectly they've come out of the pans."

I had to admit that was one good thing, but I pointed out that there was still a giant valley in the center of the cakes.

"You're right," said Mother. "I'll just take out this whole center part." She gave us both a taste and we agreed that it tasted yummy.

"But it still looks awful," I persisted. Mother wasn't discouraged yet.

"You run outside and pick some daisies," she said, "while I put the layers together and spread the frosting.

When I returned with the flowers, the freshly frosted cake really didn't look too bad. "Now," said Mother, taking a jelly jar from the cupboard, "we'll just put the daisies in the hole in the center. There—now what do you think?"

"It's the most beautiful cake in the world," I said.

I've never forgotten my mother's lesson. Life is not always full of per-fectly rounded golden brown cakes or of perfect days. But we don't have to live with failures; just face them and change them into successes. It works if you're seven or seventy-seven.

Always too soon to quit.
Never too late to start.

ANONYMOUS

A STAR IN THE APPLE

JAMES DOBSON
FROM *HOME WITH A HEART*

Some parents refer to their children as the "apple" of their eye, but one mom I know affectionately thinks of her kids as the "star" in the apple.

The mother discovered one day that by cutting an apple horizontally across the middle, instead of coring it and slicing it in wedges from top to bottom, that something new and striking appeared. A perfect five-point star was formed by the tiny seeds at the center. She'd never seen it before because she always approached the apple from a different point of view.

There's an analogy to children here that intrigues me. Most of us look at these little creatures we call kids in a certain way year after year—and we may be overlooking qualities of character that we've never seen before. We could be missing the "star" at the heart of these young lives.

If we try to see them through fresh eyes every now and then, we may stumble onto a whole new wonderful dimension to their personalities that escaped us before. So give it a try! Begin looking at your children from a new angle.

There is, I promise, a star tucked away inside every boy and girl.

CRAZY-ABOUT-ME LOVE

ELISA MORGAN AND CAROL KUYKENDALL
FROM *WHAT EVERY CHILD NEEDS*

'm going home!"

The announcement came from two houses down, where four-year-old Madeline was playing on the sidewalk with her neighborhood buddies. Sharon, sitting on her front steps, looked up from her magazine and watched as her daughter stomped up the street toward her. She soon plopped down on the step next to her, folded her chubby little arms across her chest, and stuck out her bottom lip, the way she did when she was determined not to cry.

"They don't like me," she told her mother. "They won't let me play with them." With those words, her tears came, streaking dirt down her cherub cheeks.

"Tell me what happened, Pumpkin," Sharon prompted as she wrapped her arm around her toddler.

Madeline gulp-sobbed her way through an explanation. "Jacob wouldn't let me carry his flashlight! He said I was too little and I might break it! He's so mean, Mommy! I'm *not* too little!" Exhausted from this outburst, she collapsed into the hollow of her mother's arm.

Sharon stroked her child's hair. It was so painful to see her daughter rejected and misunderstood like this. Another reminder that as a mom, she couldn't prevent the wounds her child would experience in the world. But maybe she could soften their impact with love and encouragement.

Scooping Madeline up into her lap, Sharon gently brushed her daughter's hair away from her sticky cheeks and kissed her forehead. Then she perched her daughter on her knees, held her hands, and looked straight into her wide, sad eyes, eyeball-to-eyeball.

"Madeline, do you know how wonderful you are?" she asked.

Madeline shook her head and pulled a hand free to wipe her eyes.

"Madeline, you are the most wonderful-est girl in the whole wide world! I love your button nose." Sharon smooched it quickly. "I love your cherry-red cheeks." She pecked them and continued. "I love your eyelashes and your adorable little eary ears." She bestowed kisses on her daughter's eyes and ears. "I love you from the top of your head all the way down to your twinkly little toes." She bent Madeline's head forward for a kiss and then picked up her sandaled feet and smooched her dimpled toes. "I love your heart," pointing at her chest, "your kindness, your fun ideas, your sweet little sharing spirit."

Madeline stopped crying and watched her mother, wide-eyed. She hung on to every word, giggled through the kisses, and eagerly followed from one affirmation to the next. Hungry from her very soul for these endearments, she opened, like a baby bird, to receive her mother's nurture.

Finally Sharon hugged her daughter close to her chest. "Oh, Madeline," she exclaimed, "I'm absolutely crazy about you!"

TALKING TO MY BOYS

GARY SMALLEY AND JOHN TRENT
FROM *LEAVING THE LIGHT ON*

Whenever we teach on the subject of family communication, I sometimes flash back to a scene from my high school years in our single parent home. I remember what my twin brother and I used to do when we got back from our double dates.

No matter what time we got in, whether it was 11:30 on a regular weekend, or 2:00 A.M. on prom nights, we would always go into Mom's room, flop down on either side of her on the bed, wake her up, and tell her about the evening.

Sometimes we'd lie there in the dark, talking for hours. It was like stereo for poor Mom, one twin on each side: laughing, remembering, cutting up, dreaming out loud, talking about our plans, hopes, fears, and experiences.

While I'm sure a more sensitive person would have thought of it earlier, at some point it finally dawned on us that Mom had to get up the next morning and go to work to support the family. Maybe she would prefer that we not wake her up and talk her head off on those late nights. I suggested that to her once, and I'll never forget her reply.

"John," she said, "I can always go back to sleep. But I won't always be able to talk to my boys."

Virtue

❧

MEASURING A LIFE

My deeds will be measured not by my youthful appearance,
But by the concern lines on my forehead,
The laugh lines around my mouth,
And the chins from seeing what can be done
For those smaller than me or who have fallen.

ERMA BOMBECK
FROM *FOREVER, ERMA*

LOVE NOTES

❧

DALE HANSON BOURKE
FROM *EVERYDAY MIRACLES*

*S*o *you're* the one who started all the trouble!" the well-dressed woman said to me as I introduced myself. I looked at her blankly. Standing in the middle of our children's classroom, I couldn't imagine what she was talking about.

"The notes," she declared. "I mean the notes in the children's lunchboxes. Because of your son, all the children have to have them now."

My mouth dropped open as I listened to her. I had no idea anyone even knew about the notes I tucked into Chase's lunchbox each day. But apparently he had shown them to his friends, who asked their mothers for notes, too.

I usually did my son's notes late at night before I fell into bed, or early in the morning before anyone else was awake. Blurry-eyed, I drew pictures or wrote simple words that Chase would recognize. These communiqués were my way of helping him make it through his long school day. So at lunchtime I tried to give him a little extra boost to remind him that he was special.

Now I realized the notes *had* made a difference for Chase. He felt so good about them that he had shown them to his friends. And they all wanted to feel special as well.

Each night when I cleaned out Chase's lunchbox, I would find the day's note, with greasy little fingerprints on it. It made me smile to think of him reading his note each day as he ate his lunch.

One day I opened his lunchbox to find only crumbs and a half-eaten carrot. "Where's your note, Chase?" I asked.

He looked sheepish. "Sorry, Mom," he said. "I gave it to Jimmy."

"Why?"

"Well, he never gets a note. So I thought I could share mine with him." Chase looked at me sideways, waiting for my reaction.

He was relieved when I bent down and hugged him. Jimmy's mom was single and worked long hours to support her family. I was proud my son passed his precious note on to Jimmy.

"You're a very special boy," I told him.

"I know," he responded.

All I could do was laugh. I had thought that Chase needed a note each day to remind him of that fact. Instead, he was reminding his classmates through his kindness. More importantly, he was reminding me.

Lighthouses don't ring bells and fire guns to call attention to their light…they just shine!

AUTHOR UNKNOWN

GRANNY BRAND

PAUL BRAND
FROM *IN HIS IMAGE*

One figure towers above all others who have influenced my life: my mother, known as Granny Brand. I say it kindly and in love, but in old age my mother had little of physical beauty left in her. She had been a classic beauty as a young woman—I have photographs to prove it—but not in old age. The rugged conditions in India, combined with crippling falls and her battles with typhoid, dysentery, and malaria had made her a thin, hunched-over old woman. Years of exposure to wind and sun had toughened her facial skin into leather and furrowed it with wrinkles as deep and extensive as any I have seen on a human face. She knew better than anyone that her physical appearance had long since failed her—for this reason she adamantly refused to keep a mirror in her house.

At the age of seventy-five, while working in the mountains of South India, my mother fell and broke her hip. She lay all night on the floor in pain until a workman found her the next morning. Four men carried her on a string-and-wood cot down the mountain path to the plains and put her in a jeep for an agonizing 150-mile ride over rutted roads. (She had made this trip before, after a head-first fall off a horse on a rocky mountain path, and already had experienced some paralysis below her knees.)

I soon scheduled a visit to my mother's mud-walled home in the mountains in order to persuade her to retire. By then she could walk only with the aid of two bamboo canes taller than she was, planting the canes and lifting her legs high with each painful step to keep her paralyzed feet from dragging on the ground. Yet she continued to travel on horseback and camp in the outlying villages in order to preach the gospel and treat sicknesses and pull the decayed teeth of the villagers.

I came with compelling arguments for her retirement. It was not safe for her to go on living alone in such a remote place with good help a day's journey away. With her faulty sense of balance and paralyzed legs, she presented a constant medical hazard. Already she had endured fractures of vertebrae and ribs, pressure on her spinal nerve roots, a brain concussion, a fractured femur, and severe infection of her hand. "Even the best of people do sometimes retire when they reach their seventies," I said with a smile. "Why not come to Vellore and live near us?"

Granny threw off my arguments like so much nonsense and shot back a reprimand. Who would continue the work? There was no one else in the entire mountain range to preach, to bind up wounds, and to pull teeth. "In any case," she concluded, "what is the use of preserving my old body if it is not going to be used where God needs me?"

And so she stayed. Eighteen years later, at the age of ninety-three, she reluctantly gave up sitting on her pony because she was falling all too frequently. Devoted Indian villagers began bearing her on a hammock from town to town. After two more years of mission work, she finally died at age ninety-five. She was buried, at her request, in a simple, well-used sheet laid in the ground—no coffin. She abhorred the notion of wasting precious wood on coffins. Also, she liked the symbolism of returning her physical body to its original humus even as her spirit was set free.

One of my last and strongest visual memories of my mother is set in a village in the mountains she loved, perhaps the last time I saw her in her own environment. She is sitting on a low stone wall that circles the village, with people pressing in from all sides. They are listening to all she has to say about Jesus. Heads are nodding in encouragement, and deep, searching questions come from the crowd. Granny's own rheumy eyes are shining, and standing beside her I can see what she must be seeing through failing eyes: intent faces gazing with absolute trust and affection on one they have grown to love.

I know that even with my relative youth and strength and all my specialized knowledge about health and agricultural techniques, I could never command that kind of devotion and love from these people. They are looking at a wrinkled old face, but somehow her shrunken tissues have become transparent and she is all lambent spirit. To them, she is beautiful.

Granny Brand had no need for a mirror made of glass and polished chromium; she had the incandescent faces of thousands of Indian villagers. Her worn-out physical image did nothing but enhance the image of God beaming through her like a beacon.

The best way to break a bad habit is to drop it!

ANONYMOUS

ROBERT'S CLOTHES

❦

DR. JAMES DOBSON
FROM *STRAIGHT TALK TO MEN AND THEIR WIVES*

*I*n the absence of parental leadership, some children become extremely obnoxious and defiant, especially in public places. Perhaps the best example was a ten-year-old boy named Robert, who was a patient of my good friend Dr. William Slonecker. Dr. Slonecker said his pediatric staff dreaded the days when Robert was scheduled for an office visit. He literally attacked the clinic, grabbing instruments and files and telephones. His passive mother could do little more than shake her head in bewilderment.

During one physical examination, Dr. Slonecker observed severe cavities in Robert's teeth and knew that the boy must be referred to a local dentist. But who would be given the honor? A referral like Robert could mean the end of a professional friendship. Dr. Slonecker eventually decided to send him to an older dentist who reportedly understood children. The confrontation that followed now stands as one of the classic moments in the history of human conflict.

Robert arrived in the dental office, prepared for battle.

"Get in the chair, young man!" said the doctor.

"No chance!" replied the boy.

"Son, I told you to climb onto the chair, and that's what I intend for you to do," said the dentist.

Robert stared at his opponent for a moment and then replied, "If you make me get in that chair, I will take off all my clothes."

The dentist calmly said, "Son, take 'em off." The boy forthwith removed his shirt, undershirt, shoes and socks, and then looked up in defiance.

"All right, son," said the dentist. "Now get on the chair."

"You didn't hear me," sputtered Robert. "I said if you make me get on that chair, I will take off all my clothes."

"Son, take 'em off," replied the man. Robert proceeded to remove his pants and shorts, finally standing totally naked before the dentist and his assistant.

"Now, son, get in the chair," said the doctor. Robert did as he was told, and sat cooperatively through the entire procedure. When the cavities were drilled and filled, he was instructed to step down from the chair.

"Give me my clothes now," said the boy.

"I'm sorry," replied the dentist. "Tell your mother that we're going to keep your clothes tonight. She can pick them up tomorrow."

Can you comprehend the shock Robert's mother received when the door to the waiting room opened, and there stood her pink son, as naked as the day he was born? The room was filled with patients, but Robert and his mom walked past them and into the hall. They went down a public elevator and into the parking lot, ignoring the snickers of onlookers.

The next day, Robert's mother returned to retrieve his clothes, and asked to have a word with the dentist. However, she did not come to protest. These were her sentiments: "You don't know how much I appreciate what happened here yesterday. You see, Robert has been blackmailing me about his clothes for years. Whenever we are in a public place, such as a grocery store, he makes unreasonable demands of me. If I don't immediately buy him what he wants, he threatens to take off all his clothes. You are the first person who has called his bluff, doctor, and the impact on Robert has been incredible!"

SOWING LOVE

GLADYS HUNT
FROM A SPEECH BY PASTOR DONALD EWING

The neighbors in the little house next door were a sorry lot. They were gossipy and malicious, noisy and quarrelsome. The children were addicted to the appropriation of the property of others—which is a gentle way of saying that they were a pack of junior-sized thieves. Collectively they were a thorn in the flesh of the neighborhood.

On our land but close to, and shading, their kitchen window was the most miserable skeleton of a peach tree that anyone ever saw. Every spring the gnarled old tree would, with great effort, gather together all of its little store of strength and produce a few leaves, a few blossoms. In due season the blossoms would develop into tiny, hard green peaches that never matured. They were good for only one thing—throwing. You can guess who threw them and where. It had always been so; the tree was so completely unproductive that Mother decided to have it cut down and to put flowers in its place.

It wasn't long before word of her decision reached the neighbors. They rushed over to plead with her to permit the old tree to stand because it was the only shade that they had on their kitchen. Their kitchen had a flat roof, and it was exposed to the merciless Illinois sun. It was a tempting picture, those rascals sweltering in their doubly-heated kitchen. There was certainly poetic justice in it; they had turned the heat on us often enough, and one could easily be tempted to see a prophetic element in the situation. But Mother was a Christian and believed that she ought to act like one. She said, "Of course I will leave the tree," and she did.

When spring came that year something wonderful had happened to the tree. Those bony old limbs disappeared into a great cloud of blossoms. The blossoms developed into the tiny, hard green peaches that we had known across the years, and then, wonder of wonder, they matured and became wonderful, sweet, delicious fruit.

We ate all that we could; Mother gave some away to the neighbors, including the unpleasant ones, and she canned enough to last us all through the coming year.

In a few months the neighbors moved. I do not mean to suggest that there is any connection here. But they did move; I am only reporting the facts. And that year, or the next, the tree died.

The tree had never produced good fruit before; it never produced good fruit again: it did so just that one year. I know what some of you are thinking—the tree would have produced fruit even if Mother had not been so nice; it was something about the season or the chemicals. I don't know why it happened; I do not claim to. But I do know this: if she had returned evil for evil, it would not have happened for there would have been no tree, and a small boy would have missed one of the most beautiful experiences and one of the deepest lessons of his whole life.

Mother had an opportunity to get even and instead, she sowed love, and there came forth a wonderful harvest. There was a harvest on the tree but there was also a harvest in her soul, in mine, in many others.

THAT WAS A BEAUTIFUL WOMAN

SANDY SNAVELY

While browsing through some old photographs I came across a picture of a young woman on a beach. Her face looked familiar. I stared at her for a moment and then was startled to recognize the attractive girl, running through the waves without a wrinkle on her face. She was me. A momentary wave of sadness swept over my heart as I realized how quickly time had passed and how impartial the aging process had been.

Some faces are easily forgotten, yet there is one face that can never be erased from my memory. Hers was one of the most beautiful faces I have ever seen.

I met her in a convalescent home where I had been asked to come to entertain the elderly patients who resided there. As I wandered from room to room, my colorful wig, big floppy shoes, and red rubber nose stood in stark contrast to the cruel consequences of growing old. There, in one of those tiny rooms, I discovered the woman who redefined my image of beauty.

Her frail body lay imprisoned by the bars of a hospital bed. Long strands of snow white hair webbed across the crisp cotton pillow that cradled her head. Ivory skin clung tightly to her perfectly sculptured cheekbones and delicate chin. The woman's slender fingers pulled my face close to hers. It was then that our eyes met and the reflection of her soul captivated my attention. With my ear close to her lips she sang to me the finale of her life's story. "Jesus, Jesus, oh, how I love Him."

There was a gentle boldness to her words. I felt small standing next to her in my silly disguise. I thought I was there to bring joy to people whose lives were nearing an end. Instead she brought joy to me.

Her words were sung as a testimony to the loveliness of the woman who still resided in the heart of the body that was quickly withering away. Unwittingly she left a legacy of beauty that still sings its quiet message to my heart.

Photographs can only tell a portion of the story, but our hearts will reveal the true value of our lives. Perhaps one day when my children grow up they will thumb through our old family albums. I hope they will be captivated not by that young, unwrinkled girl romping in the waves but by the mature face of the woman they knew as their mother. On that day, I hope they will see beyond the aging face in the pictures and say, "That was a beautiful woman."

Never report what may hurt another unless
it be a greater hurt to some other to conceal it.

WILLIAM PENN

THE PAPER HEART

GIGI GRAHAM TCHIVIDJIAN
FROM *CURRENTS OF THE HEART*

Our voices rose along with the intensity of the argument.

We exchanged words we didn't mean. We threw out issues that weren't relevant. We rehashed past grievances, forgiven but never forgotten.

Neither of us had intended our simple discussion to accelerate into a heated argument.

It was late, and both of us were tired. Too tired. Stephan and I had both endured a day-long parade of stress, tensions, and mini-crises. I'd found myself pulled in ten different directions all day: the children, laundry, groceries, writing deadlines, friends wanting advice, letters needing answers, the jangling telephone. I felt fragmented and weary beyond description.

Stephan, too, had experienced an especially trying day, dealing with men and women whose lives were falling apart. After an hour of fighting traffic he arrived at home to find children clamoring for his attention, a list of patients to call, and a stack of bills to be paid. All evening we had been living on the edge of a scream, trying to control our frayed nerves.

Then a minor disagreement accelerated way out of control.

As our words heated the air, the door to our bedroom cracked open.

Slowly. Quietly. A small hand reached through the opening and placed something on the door. Then just as quietly the hand retreated and the door closed. Curious, I got up to investigate. Taped to the door I found a small paper heart colored with red crayon and emblazoned with the words "I love Mom and Dad."

Eight-year-old Anthony was doing his part to try to make peace.

Suddenly I remembered the verse, "A little child shall lead them" (Isaiah 11:6, KJV). Shame-filled tears trickled down my face. Stephan and I looked at each other, both sorry for the way we had allowed our over-taxed emotions to control us and to upset our home....

I can't even remember what Stephan and I were arguing about when little Anthony placed his paper heart on our bedroom door.

But we have left it there as a reminder.

The most loved folks in our community seem to be the ones
who never can recall anything bad about any of us.

AUTHOR UNKNOWN
FROM *LIFE LESSONS*

A CHRISTMAS TRADITION

༄

PAT A. CARMAN

n keeping with the holiday tradition, our office searched for a family that may not have a Christmas without some assistance. We contacted several agencies and churches, and at last found a family of eight who had experienced not just one year of misfortune, but several. Living in a small Oregon town in the foothills of the Cascades, the personal tragedies they had experienced in the previous two years had forced them to begin all over again financially. They expected their holidays would be sparse and pretty bleak! But what they lacked in material possessions they made up for in their strong sense of family and love for each other.

For one month we gathered gifts in brightly wrapped boxes and packages and cash donations in a decorated tin. As we shopped for Mom, Dad, and these six children we had such fun deciding just what each would get, and we could just envision their Christmas morning when they would unwrap the gifts! For the boys we bought warm winter gloves for snowy days when they walked to school and models to put together when housebound. For the little girls, pretty dolls and fuzzy animal slippers. For the oldest daughter in her early teens, some perfume and a watch. Dad would receive a new ski sweater, to remind him that he needed to take time from work in his studio to have fun on the nearby slopes.

And, for Mom, a much-deserved new Christmas outfit. Our gift for the whole family was a game for all to enjoy and we also added the makings of a Christmas dinner.

The family would not know, of course, who their own personal Santas had been. We made arrangements for the pastor of their small country church to deliver our presents several days before Christmas. We would ship the gifts to him, from our town 120 miles away, thus remaining anonymous.

Our excitement was building and we waited in anticipation to hear "the rest of the story," but not one of us could have guessed what really happened. We found out later we were not the only characters in this story.

On the Friday before Christmas, the mother of our family came home from work. Employed as a software engineer in a nearby town, she excitedly announced that her employer had given her a $300 Christmas bonus. Her husband welcomed the news. Now they had money to provide a Christmas for the children! Together they composed a list, making sure that the "wants" equaled the "needs." They would do some shopping next week, in the two days before the holiday. What a timely gift!

That weekend, as a family they attended their Sunday church service, feeling a great release from pressure. In a special prayer time they heard that one of their friends from the congregation was soon to have surgery. He was out of work and unable to pay medical bills and his family was without food. Knowing the desperation their friends must feel, they felt an immediate sympathy to their situation. When they returned home, they held a "family meeting" and decided as a group to give their Christmas bonus to their friends. Food and medical bills were more important than Christmas toys.

Within a few hours after making their decision, the pastor stopped by to visit his longtime friends. Before he could explain the reason for the day's visit, they told him they would like to donate their good fortune, and asked him to deliver a check for them. The pastor was amazed at their generosity and agreed to deliver the check if the family would come out to his car with him. Puzzled, but agreeable, they walked to the driveway where they found his car overflowing with Christmas presents—the presents we sent over the mountains as our expression of Christmas love. What an awesome Christmas it was, for all of us, that year!

SECOND FIDDLE

Someone once asked the conductor of a great symphony orchestra which instrument he considered the most difficult to play.

"Second fiddle," said the conductor. "I can get plenty of first violinists, but to find one who can play second fiddle with enthusiasm—that's a problem. And if we have no second fiddle, we have no harmony!"

AUTHOR UNKNOWN
FROM *MORE OF…THE BEST OF BITS AND PIECES*

MOTHER TERESA'S ANSWER

❧

DR. PAUL BRAND AND PHILIP YANCEY
FROM *FEARFULLY AND WONDERFULLY MADE*

simple woman named Mother Teresa has been awarded a Nobel Peace Prize for her work in Calcutta among members of India's lowest caste. She cannot save all India, so she seeks the least redeemable, the dying. When she finds them, in the gutters and garbage dumps of Calcutta's alleys, she brings them to her hospital and surrounds them with love. Smiling women daub at their sores, clean off layers of grime, and swaddle them in soft sheets. The beggars, often too weak to talk, stare wide-eyed at this seemingly misdirected love offered so late in their lives. Have they died and gone to heaven? Why this sudden outpouring of care—why the warm, strengthening broth being gently spooned to their mouths?

A newsman in New York—properly outfitted in a three-piece suit, taking cues from an off-camera TelePrompTer—confronted Mother Teresa with a similar line of questioning. He seemed pleased with his acerbic probing. Why indeed should she expend her limited resources on people for whom there was no hope? Why not attend to people worthy of rehabilitation? What kind of success rate could her hospital boast of when most of its patients died in a matter of days or weeks? Mother Teresa stared at him in silence, absorbing the questions, trying to pierce through the façade to discern what kind of a man would ask them. She had no answers that would make sense to him, so she said softly, "These people have been treated all their lives like dogs. Their greatest disease is a sense that they are unwanted. Don't they have the right to die like angels?"

Lord,
I renounce my desire for human praise,
For the approval of my peers,
The need for public recognition.

I deliberately put these aside today,
Content to hear you whisper,
"Well done, my faithful servant."

Amen.

FINDERS, KEEPERS

FAITH ANDREWS BEDFORD
FROM *COUNTRY LIVING* MAGAZINE

orty years ago on a hot, August day I first experienced what it must be like to be wealthy. Mother needed milk so I volunteered to ride my bike to the village and fetch some.

As I passed the school, its swings hung still and silent; the seesaws shimmered in the afternoon sunshine. Soon this quiet place would be full of laughter and squeals. Seesaws would squeak and swings would arc against the sky, their chains clattering as children pumped them high into the air. In a little more than a month, my sisters and I would walk through the big stone gates, new shoes gleaming, new notebooks held tightly. I would be entering the sixth grade, the highest grade in the school, and I was going to be on the safety patrol.

As I came to the edge of the village, I pedaled faster. I'd been saving up to buy the little horses in Mrs. Bridges' toy shop window and was eager to see if they were still there. I only had $4.25 left to save until they would be mine.

Ahead was the toy store and there, in the window, was the little horse family. The black stallion reared up; the palomino mare bent down as if to graze; their little foal stood alert. I had long imagined how the trio would look on my bureau top; I would cut fresh grass every day and arrange it beneath the mare's muzzle.

Still dreaming of the horses, I nearly stepped on a lump of paper. I bent down and realized it was a roll of money. I picked it up. *It must be hundreds,* I thought, *millions!* I raced around the corner toward the grocery store, almost knocking over our neighbor Mr. Peabody.

"Look!" I said, waving the roll wildly in the air. "Look what I just found!"

"Well, well, well," Mr. Peabody said. "That's quite a find. But you need to be more careful with that bike, young lady," he scowled with mock ferocity.

"Yes, sir," I said breathlessly and pushed on, a little more slowly this time. I leaned my bike against a tree and dashed into the store. The coldness of the milk bottle felt good against my skin as I stood fidgeting in the checkout line. Pushing my bike back toward the toy store, I returned to the magic spot where I'd found the money. The street was still empty; I saw no one around.

I burst into the toy shop. The little bell on the shop's door clanged wildly and Mrs. Bridges turned around with a start. "Goodness, Faith!" she gasped, her hand flying to her throat. "Whatever is the matter?"

"Nothing," I grinned, waving the roll of bills gaily. "I've come to buy the little horses. I'm sure there's enough here."

"My, my. There certainly does seem to be. Let's count it."

Mrs. Bridges carefully counted out three tens and an endless number of ones. "You've got $47 here, dear," she said with surprise. "Last week you told me you had eight saved up."

"Yes," I said. "But now I'm rich!"

Mrs. Bridges smiled and retrieved the little horses from the window and put them in a bag. I took it and ran out the door shouting a thank-you over my shoulder.

The milk bottle rattled in my bike basket as I raced home. I dashed through the kitchen door just in time to find Mother hanging up the phone.

"Mother, I found a whole bunch of money!" I shouted hugging her excitedly.

"I know," she said softly.

"You do? How?"

"That was Mr. Peabody on the phone. He told me he'd bumped into you in the village. Literally." I could feel my face redden as I recalled nearly toppling him.

"He told me about your having found the money. Then he told me he met the lady who lost it."

The heat of the day disappeared as a chill descended upon me.

"No." I whispered, tears welling up in my eyes. "It's mine."

"Faith, Faith," Mother said as she drew me close. "Mr. Peabody said that when he came out of the bank, he saw a mother with her little boy frantically searching the sidewalk in front of the electric company. When he asked her if she'd lost something she said that she'd put the money to pay her electric bill in one pocket and her grocery money in the other. When she went in to pay her bill, the money was gone. The clerk told her they would cut off her electricity if she couldn't pay. She was desperate, Mr. Peabody said. It was a good thing he saw her."

"No it wasn't," I cried as I buried my face in Mother's shoulder.

"There, there," she said, patting me gently. "You need to hush now. The lady will be here soon. Mr. Peabody told her where we live."

"But I found it," I shouted, pulling away from Mother's embrace. "Finders, keepers."

Mother just looked at me.

"And besides," I sobbed, clutching the paper sack tightly, "I bought the little horses with some of that money."

"Well," Mother said quietly, stroking my hair, "I guess you'll have to take them back."

I sniffed and reluctantly realized that she was right. The money had never been mine. Not really. I knew I had done nothing to earn it. The pleasure of owning the little horses was beginning to dim. The sack grew heavy in my hands.

By the time I heard the soft knock at the door, I had stopped crying and had washed my face with cold water. I heard a woman's voice say, "Are you Mrs. Andrews? I think your daughter may have found the money I lost. Forty-seven dollars?" I peeked around the corner and saw Mother open the screen door.

"You have the right house," Mother replied. "Come in. You've had a long walk. Won't you have some lemonade?" The woman nodded. Her thin dress clung to her in the heat. One hand held a bag of groceries and the other rested on the shoulder of a skinny little boy. I had stood behind them in line at the grocery store.

Mother saw me. "This is Faith," she said, motioning me forward. "She's the one who found your money."

"In front of the electric company?" the woman asked. I nodded silently.

"Forty-seven dollars?"

"Yes," I said slowly, handing her the rest of her money, plus the eight dollars from my piggy bank. Relief spread across her pale face like sunshine after a rain.

"Oh, thank you," she said. "I was so frightened. I just didn't know where I was going to come up with the money to pay our bill."

"It's not all there," I mumbled in embarrassment.

"Excuse me?" she said, not quite catching my words.

"I spent some," I said, hanging my head.

"Oh," she laughed. "I'd planned to give you a five-dollar reward for finding my money and keeping it safe for me. Did you spend that much?"

I shook my head. "No, ma'am, I didn't. I only spent $4.25."

"Then here," she said, dropping three quarters into my open hand. "Here's the rest of your reward." Her little boy looked at me with wide eyes.

Mother and the lady sat in the parlor sipping lemonade and talking about this and that: the weather, the county fair, the start of school. I showed her son how to play Chinese checkers.

Then I heard the lady say, "William will be in first grade this year."

"You will?" I asked him. He moved one of his marbles into place and nodded shyly. He looked both proud and scared.

"Here," I said, pressing one of my reward quarters into his hand. "You'll need some colored pencils," I advised, feeling at once wise and magnanimous. After all, I'd been wealthy for a brief moment. And now that I had my little horses, all my needs were met.

The day had begun to cool by the time William and his mother left for home. I stood in our front yard and watched them turn down the lane. Then I began to pick a bit of fresh grass for my little horses.

Just before they turned the corner, I heard William call out a good-bye and thank-you. One hand was held in his mother's, but he waved the other in farewell. It was still clasped around his quarter. I could tell he didn't trust pockets.

If you are all wrapped up in yourself, you are way overdressed.

JANE ANN CLARK

ARE WE RICH?

ERMA BOMBECK
FROM *FOREVER, ERMA*

The other day out of a clear blue sky Brucie asked, "Are we rich?"

I paused on my knees as I retrieved a dime from the sweeper bag, blew the dust off it and asked, "Not so you can notice. Why?"

"How can you tell?" he asked.

I straightened up and thought a bit. Being rich is a relative sort of thing. Here's how I can always tell.

"You're rich when you buy your gas at the same service station all the time so your glasses match.

"You're rich when you can have eight people to dinner and don't have to wash forks between the main course and dessert.

"You're rich when you buy clothes for your kids that are two sizes too big for the one you buy 'em for and four sizes too big for the one that comes after him.

"You're rich when you own a boat—without oars.

"You can tell people have money when they record a check and don't have to subtract it right away.

"People have money when they sit around and joke with the cashier while she's calling in their charge to see if it's still open.

"You're rich when you write notes to the teacher on paper without lines.

"You're rich when your television set has all the knobs on it.

"You're rich when you can throw away a pair of pantyhose just because it has a large hole in it.

"You know people are loaded when they don't have to save rubber bands from the celery and store them on a doorknob.

"You're rich when you can have a home wedding without HAVEN FUNERAL HOME stamped on the folding chairs.

"You're rich when the Scouts have a paper drive and you have a stack of *The New York Times* in your basement.

"You're rich when your dog is wet and smells good.

"You're rich when your own hair looks so great everyone thinks it's a wig."

Brucie sat quietly for a moment, then said, "I think my friend Ronny is rich."

"How can you tell?" I asked.

"His mom buys his birthday cake at a bakery, and it isn't even cracked on top."

"He's rich, all right," I sighed.

MARGARET OF NEW ORLEANS

SARA CONE BRYANT

f you ever go to the beautiful city of New Orleans, somebody will be sure to take you down into the old business part of the city, where there are banks and shops and hotels, and show you a statue erected in 1884 which stands in a little square there. It is the statue of a woman, sitting in a low chair, with her arms around a child, who leans against her. The woman is not at all pretty. She wears thick, common shoes, a plain dress, with a little shawl, and a sunbonnet. She is stout and short, and her face is a square-chinned Irish face. But her eyes look at you like your mother's.

It is the statue of a woman named Margaret. Her whole name was Margaret Haughery, but no one in New Orleans remembers her by it, any more than you think of your dearest sister by her full name. She is just Margaret. This is her story, and it tells why people made a monument for her.

When Margaret was a tiny baby, her father and mother died, and she was adopted by two young people as poor and as kind as her own parents. She lived with them until she grew up. Then she married, and had a little baby of her own. But very soon her husband died, and then the baby died, too, and Margaret was all alone in the world. She was poor, but she was strong, and knew how to work.

All day, from morning until evening, she ironed clothes in a laundry. And every day, as she worked by the window, she saw the little motherless children from the orphanage nearby working and playing about. After a while, a great sickness came upon the city, and so many mothers and fathers died that there were more orphans than the orphanage could possibly take care of. They needed a good friend now. You would hardly think, would you, that a poor woman who worked in a laundry could be much of a friend to them? But Margaret was. She went straight to the kind Sisters who ran the orphanage and told them she was going to give them part of her wages and was going to work for them, besides. Pretty soon she had worked so hard that she had some money saved from her wages. With this, she bought two cows and a little delivery cart. Then she carried her milk to her customers in the little cart every morning, and as she went, she begged the leftover food from the hotels and rich houses, and brought it back in the cart to the hungry children in the orphanage. In the very hardest times that was often all the food the children had.

A part of the money Margaret earned every week went to the orphanage, and after a few years it was made very much larger and better. And Margaret was so careful and so good at business that, in spite of her giving, she bought more cows and earned more money. With this, she built a home for orphan babies; she called it her baby house.

After a time, Margaret had a chance to get a bakery, and then she became a bread-woman instead of a milk-woman. She carried the bread just as she had carried the milk, in her cart. And still she kept giving money to the orphanage. Then the great war came, the Civil War. In all the trouble and sickness and fear of that time, Margaret drove her cart of bread, and somehow she had always enough to give the starving soldiers, and for her babies, besides what she sold. And despite all this, she earned enough so that when the war was over she built a big steam factory for her bread. By this time everybody in the city knew her. The children all over the city loved her. The businessmen were proud of her. The poor people all came to her for advice. She used to sit at the open door of her office, in a calico gown and a little shawl, and give a good word to everybody, rich or poor.

Then, one day, Margaret died. And when it was time to read her will, the people found that, with all her giving she had still saved a great deal of money, $30,000!, and that she had left every cent of it to the different orphanages of the city—each one of them was given something. Whether they were for white children or black, for Jews, Catholics, or Protestants, made no difference; for Margaret always said, "They are all orphans alike." And just think, that splendid, wise will was signed with a cross instead of a name, for Margaret had never learned to read or write!

When the people of New Orleans learned that Margaret was dead, they said, "She was a mother to the motherless. She was a friend to those who had no friends. She had wisdom greater than schools can teach. We will not let her memory go from us." So they made a statue of her, just as she used to look, sitting in her own office door, or driving in her own little cart. And there it stands today, in memory of the great love and the great power of plain Margaret Haughery, of New Orleans.

LET IT SHINE!

CHERYL KIRKING

Now it's time to go to sleep!" I said as I tried to exit my three-year-old triplets' room. I had already told three stories, listened to three very long prayers, kissed three teddy bears, a bunny and kangaroo good night. I had gotten three glasses of water and subsequently made three trips to the bathroom.

"But Mommy," Bryce pleaded, "I've gotta tell you something important!"

"Go to sleep!" I replied firmly.

"But Mommy, it's really important…you gotta come here!"

"What is it, Bryce?" I asked.

"You hafta come here!" he persisted.

"What is it, Bryce?" I repeated, kneeling beside his little toddler bed. Taking my face in his soft, dimpled hands, he looked me in the eyes and whispered, "Mommy, don't ever hide your light under a biscuit!"

I assured him that I would not.

"He means basket," Sarah Jean explained from across the room. "Our Sunday school teacher said a bushel is a kind of basket."

"Yes," offered Blake from the third little bed. "We sang about that," and he broke into an enthusiastic rendition of "This Little Light of Mine," complete with actions to the verse "Hide it under a bushel...NO!"

"That's right, Mommy," Bryce repeated solemnly, once again cradling my face in his hands. "Don't you ever hide your light under a biscuit! Let it shine, let it shine, let it shine!"

After one more glass of water and three more kisses, I finally made it back downstairs to enjoy a quiet moment over a cup of tea and muse over the night's bedtime remarks.

I thought of times that I had failed to serve others because I wasn't paying attention to their needs. I recalled times that I had "held back" because I felt insecure about my abilities, and in so doing missed out on opportunities to let my light shine. And I prayed that God might help me and my children to discover and offer our "little lights" to others, never hiding them under bushels...or, for that matter, biscuits!

RANDOM ACTS
OF KINDNESS

THE EDITORS OF CONARI PRESS
FROM *RANDOM ACTS OF KINDNESS*

One Friday afternoon I was on my way to set up for a book fair in San Francisco. Waiting at a stoplight in front of the convention center, I noticed a handicapped woman on the street corner. She was sitting against a fence, a walker by her side, surrounded by what was probably all of her belongings.

As I watched, another woman, perfectly coifed, in high heels and a power suit, came up to her with a bag. Without a word, the business-woman proceeded to lay out prepared food which she had obviously bought "to go," around the street person so that she could easily reach the food from a sitting position. The homeless woman looked on in grateful amazement, as if her guardian angel had appeared out of nowhere, just in time. In fact, she had.

Three days later, when I was leaving the convention center, I passed the same woman leaning against the same fence. This time a man in a van was at the stoplight, honking and holding money out to the woman. She was trying to move, but couldn't get up. Quickly, I ran to the van, grabbed the money, and brought it to her. I felt so happy to see people taking care of this woman, and pleased that my weekend was bracketed by tokens of generosity.

WINGS

KATHERINE G. BOND
FROM *FOCUS ON THE FAMILY CLUBHOUSE* MAGAZINE

Miranda Jane Lonneker, age ten and three-quarters, gazed at the flock of model airplanes suspended from her brother's ceiling. Perched on her shoulder, her goldfinch Chester looked too.

George didn't want her in his room, especially when he was gone. "It's his own fault," she told Chester. "I wouldn't be here if we were buying each other's Christmas presents at the five and dime."

But George had forgotten about their annual tradition. Instead he'd gone caroling with "the fellows," one last bash to finish out 1936. She'd begged to go along, but George's buddies had given him "that look."

"Maybe another time, Sis," he'd said.

"Another time," she fumed. Chester rubbed his silky head against her, seeming to understand. Two summers ago, she'd rescued Chester from the neighbor's cat. His wing had healed crooked, so he flew now in a strange, looping fashion.

Miranda touched the Curtiss Jenny, a hand-carved, two-seater biplane. Her favorite, though it had no wings. George was still waiting for them.

On George's fifth birthday, a barnstormer uncle had taken him and Father up in a Jenny while Mother wasn't looking.

Someone had taken a photograph of their landing, George crowing joyously, fist in the air; Mother scowling on the ground. After that glorious flight, Mother declared Father and George grounded. Two months later, George said, the government grounded the Jenny, declaring it unsafe.

The uncle had given George the Jenny, promising the wings on his next trip. But there had never been a next trip.

Every birthday George waited and talked about his "pilot-uncle" until one year Mother exclaimed, "You uncle is a reckless fool." George had never mentioned him again. Meanwhile, the Jenny perched, like a clipped bird on George's dresser.

George had told Miranda about the day he fell in love with the airplane so many times it was almost her own memory.

Secretly, she dreamed of taking off, like Amelia Earhart, but Mother believed flying was not suitable for a lady.

Maybe it didn't matter that George had missed their date. "He could never give me what I *really* want," she told Chester. She spun the propeller of the Jenny. "He'd never give it up."

At that moment George strode in. "For crying out loud Miranda, get your hands off my Jenny!"

Miranda's cheeks went hot.

"It's not enough for you to follow me everywhere; you've got to be fooling with my planes whenever I'm gone."

Miranda fled, Chester still gripping her shoulder.

Maybe George had forgotten about *her* present, but she and Chester could go without him. She hoped he felt lousy when she gave him *his* present.

The yard was dotted with puddles. No snow for Christmas, just gray Northwest sky. The gate hung by one hinge; paint flaked off as she opened it. The fence embarrassed Mother but paint and hardware cost money.

Chester fluttered behind as Miranda tramped past the train station.

"Hello there."

Miranda looked around.

"Miranda, isn't it?" On the station platform sat the owner of the voice, a man in a straw hat. One of his eyes was sky blue; the other was made of glass. He was whittling as he sat.

"Hello, Sir," Miranda remembered her manners. "I don't believe I know your name."

"My name?" He looked at the sky. "It's Jack, Miss—Daredevil Jack, they used to call me—but just plain Jack will do for now."

"I'm pleased to meet you Mr., uh, Jack." The name did not ring a bell, yet he'd called her Miranda. "Are you from around here?"

"I'm from wherever the train takes me. That's a fine bird you've got."

As if to get a closer look, Chester gave a warbling chirrup and landed on Jack's knee. Jack cocked his head and chirruped back. "Wouldn't think of selling him now, would you?" he asked.

"Sell Chester? I'd sooner sell my brother."

Jack laughed. Chester hopped onto his hand.

"You sure have a way with birds." Miranda shifted from one foot to the other. "Chester doesn't usually take to strangers."

"Finches are a favorite of mine. There's something about this one, though." Jack ran a finger over Chester's crooked wing. "Perhaps we're kindred spirits."

He held the bird out to her. Miranda scooped him back and tucked him inside her coat. "I guess I'd better be going," she said.

"Indeed." He went back to his whittling. "But don't forget to tell your brother, George, that Jack is back."

Miranda stopped. "George isn't much of a brother," she blurted.

"Ahhh." Jack's good eye gleamed. "It's these he's needing." He held up his carving. It was wings, biplane wings, the wings of a Jenny.

Miranda sucked in her breath. "How did you know? Can I take them?"

"Well, now Miss, these have a price. Yes, there's always a price for wings."

"How much?" It was important suddenly that she possess something that George wanted badly.

"How much are you willing to give?"

A strange question. It caught Miranda off guard. She pulled out the coins in her pocket. Twenty-seven cents. Jack shook his head.

"Not much to give up."

Miranda flashed hot. "It's all I have! I cleaned the cellar all day for it."

"Ah, but you could get it again." He flew the wings past his good eye.

"When you fly it's just you and the sky. These wings, they're sturdy enough to walk on and you just step out from the cockpit. It's cold with the wind whipping, and you're hanging onto the struts for dear life, but oh—the countryside is spread out like a quilt and you want to shout for the joy of it. It's a mighty thing."

Miranda imagined Jack standing on the wing of a Jenny, while the crowd below held its breath. She felt that way about George: as if he was wingwalking high above her, as if he'd never come down.

Jack set the wings aside. "You're crying, Miss."

Chester rubbed his head against Miranda's wet cheek. "What happened to your eye?" she asked.

"Let's just say that Jack's daredevil days are past." He gazed at the sky. "But what about your George? Sounds like you want to keep him on the ground."

Miranda looked up, startled. "No, I—how could I? He doesn't even love me."

"Ah, Miss Miranda, just because a man needs to fly doesn't mean he'll never land."

A man. Her brother wasn't a man. She wanted him to build her forts and help her dig worms for Chester. Instead he was off with his buddies, or behind his closed door.

"I had a sister once," said Jack. "She loved me as much as you love George. She loved me so much she put a cage around me and all I could see was the bars."

Miranda felt Chester's heart fluttering against her chest. "So what did you do?"

"I flew away," he said softly. "I flew far away."

Miranda looked at the Jenny wings. Always a price, Jack had said. She swallowed. "A trade?" She kissed Chester's soft feathers. "Wings for wings?" Chester flew to Jack's shoulder, as if he belonged there.

"Come for Christmas!" She cried impulsively. "Nobody should be alone at Christmas."

Jack stroked Chester. "I'm not alone now, am I? Thank you kindly, Miranda, but I've done what I came to do." He placed the wings in her hands, saluted and walked into the station.

When Miranda brought her package to George his eyes grew wide. He lifted the wings as if they'd come from an ancient treasure chest. "How did you manage this?"

"I bought them," she said, "from Jack."

"Uncle Jack's back? Where?!"

"At the station, he's—I think he's leaving on the evening train."

George looked at the clock and flew out of the house.

When George and the wanderer came home the spoons in Mother's hand clattered to the floor. "Jack," she whispered, her eyes shining.

George crossed the room and placed a package in Miranda's lap. She lifted the lid. There, nestled in flannel, was the wingless Jenny.

Miranda couldn't speak. She started to laugh. George laughed with her, a deep rumble, almost a man's laugh. Suddenly, she knew what real love was. It was giving somebody wings.

Motherhood

THE HANDPRINT

Sometimes you get discouraged
Because I am so small
And always leave my fingerprints
On furniture and walls.

But every day I'm growing—
I'll be all grown up someday
And those tiny little handprints
Will surely fade away.

So here's a special handprint
Just so you'll recall
Exactly how my fingers looked
When I was very small.

WRITTEN ON A PLAQUE WITH OUR GRANDDAUGHTER'S
HANDPRINT WHEN SHE WAS FIVE YEARS OLD

LOOK AT ALL THOSE WEEDS!

CINDY ROSENE DEADRICK
FROM *COUNTRY LIVING* MAGAZINE

*B*eauty is in the eye of the beholder," as the old saying goes, and so I am reminded by my three-year-old daughter as she erupts into screams of delight at the sight of our front yard abloom with a multitude of riotous dandelions. "Sunflowers!" she shouts. Eagerly, she recruits her two-year-old sister to assist in gathering a bouquet for Mom. Hand in hand, they dash about the yard, hardly knowing where to start, each sunny blossom as enticing as the next. After several minutes they return, each clutching a handful of twisted stems with golden heads, which they thrust into my reluctant palm.

"Put them on your desk, Mommy—in a cup of water in case they get thirsty," my preschooler instructs me. I don't have the heart to tell my daughters that their newfound treasures are only present on our lawn because their father applied the wrong kind of weed killer.

"I'll bet there'll be lots more when we come home tonight," she tells me, unable to contain her excitement. She has no idea just how many hundreds more will appear. Certainly dandelions have a way of multiplying that defies logic. Indeed, our entire two-acre lot will soon be awash in a yellow sea, not a blade of grass visible to the eye, and our usually friendly neighbors will be secretly scorning us for contaminating the entire block with the invasive yellow flowers. The county Weed Board will probably want us to be the poster family in their "Control Obnoxious Weeds" campaign.

Over the course of the next week, my two darlings continue to delight in their morning garden-tending duties, beginning each day with a dandelion-picking session and happily bestowing their floral gifts on a succession of their favorite people: Daddy, Grandma, their day-care provider—even the family mutt. His kennel has never looked better than it does now, graced with a flurry of canary-colored blooms.

As we drive through town going about our daily routine, our car is filled with shouts of glee as my little Dandelion Patrol Girls spy yet another yard filled with the glorious golden interloper. Elated at their good fortune in finding still more of the wondrous weed, they beg me to stop and let them gather a few more stems.

In their infinite capacity to simply enjoy life, my two young offspring gradually bring me to an attitude adjustment. "Why not take time to stop and pick the dandelions?" I finally ask myself. Who dictated that humans shouldn't enjoy certain varieties of flowers unless they are properly contained? It was probably the idea of some chemical company seeking to increase sales. But the joy we take in a jolt of vibrant color after a long, gray winter shouldn't be diminished just because some unknown arbiter of landscape fashion has decreed that a blush of gold spoils the look of a well-groomed lawn.

So, while my husband is consulting with the chemical expert at our local lawn and garden center, trying to determine what went awry in his carefully conceived weed-control plan, I have joined in the fun with my daughters. My workday is brightened by five lemony blooms winking at me from a small jar on my desk, and I have a renewed, childlike appreciation for the natural beauty all around me. I am determined to slow down and take notice of all the simple pleasures nature has in store. The other day when my daughter filled her pocket with shiny pebbles she found in the driveway, she told me she found diamonds. And I believed her.

THE WISH
BENEATH MY PILLOW

ROBIN JONES GUNN
FROM *MOTHERING BY HEART*

he kids were both at school today when I found my wish. I was cleaning closets and discovered a small, unmarked box on my son's top shelf. I placed it on the edge of the bed. It toppled over, spilling its contents onto the floor. The first thing I saw was a tiny blue tennis shoe. "His first pair of running Nikes" my brother had written on the gift card. I picked up the unbelievably small shoe and held it in the palm of my hand. I couldn't help but compare. Reaching inside the closet, I extracted one smelly high-top tennis shoe, big boy's size two. I held them next to each other. The contrast was mind-boggling.

That night I looked at my nine-year-old's feet as he came to the dinner table. I stared at them tucked under the table as he did his homework. I watched him walk up the stairs. When I tucked him in bed, I grabbed his right foot and gave it a playful wrangle. It no longer fit in the palm of my hand.

After the kids were asleep, I slipped upstairs and retrieved the baby shoe I'd hidden among my socks that afternoon. Nobody saw me press the silly little thing to my cheek and then tuck it under my pillow.

Ross and I went to bed several hours later. I curled up next to my warm husband and slipped my hand between the cool sheets and my pillowcase.

It was still there. I clutched the tiny shoes, closed my eyes, held my breath, and made a wish.

What did I wish? I'll never tell. But it might have something to do with a pair of feet that could fit in these shoes.

COLLEGE-BOUND BLESSING

I have held you close. Now as you fly into adulthood, bound to open books and discover new worlds, I release you. But not without one final prayer—prosper not only in your studies, but prosper in knowing God more richly.

I will not be there to catch you when you fall. But God will catch you when I can't. Depend on Him and learn to trust Him. You are not alone. Knowing this, my empty nest will not seem so lonely. My heart will soar as I watch you take wing.

LINDA E. SHEPHERD
FROM *LOVE'S LITTLE RECIPES FOR LIFE*

TO WHOM IT MAY CONCERN

INA HUGHS
FROM *A PRAYER FOR CHILDREN*

Wouldn't it be nice if a mom could send her child out into the world with a list of instructions and a guarantee? The day they set out for kindergarten, all slicked up in a new outfit and carrying shiny new lunch boxes, if we mothers who smile and sniff back at the bus stop had our "druthers," we'd send along a letter that goes something like this:

To Whom It May Concern, and I Sure Hope It Does:

> This is a very special little five-year-old girl. She is especially special to her father, who is still mumbling incoherently about where all the time has gone.
>
> It seems like only yesterday when she spent her mornings flopping around in my shoes and watching *Captain Kangaroo.* However, if you know a few important things about her, I am sure she will love school as much as I did a hundred years ago.
>
> Whenever she gets hurt or upset, she gets a stomach ache. The best remedy is to put her on your lap and kiss her three times—on the cheek, neck, and forehead.

Just a little family ritual perhaps you should know about. She likes to be called Snicklefritz, her daddy's pet name for her, which might come in handy if she gets homesick.

As for lunch, she doesn't like spinach, squash, asparagus, cooked carrots, yams (only sweet potatoes with marshmallows), beets, veal, or potato salad. She likes hot dogs (no mustard), hamburgers (with mayonnaise), soup (Campbell's Chicken & Stars), pizza (plain), and peanut butter (not the generic kind and never crunchy). Please add a teaspoon of sugar to her milk or else she will make a horrible face and may spit it out.

Her lunch money will be in a little purse around her neck. She knows her quarters from her nickels, but dimes give her a fit. Just remind her a dime is the thing she swallowed once. If she ever should lose her money, please don't let her go hungry. We have MasterCard and Visa.

She forgets sometimes that she needs to go to the bathroom, but you can usually tell by the way she stands. She doesn't like to wash her hands before lunch, so will you patiently remind her about ten times?

Should there ever be a thunderstorm during school, please hold her hand and make jokes about how the angels must be bowling in heaven. I know that's not very scientific, but it helps. You'll probably need to comb her hair every day after recess. Please use only covered rubber bands, and I'm sure you can tell that it looks better parted on the left.

She's very worried about carrying her own lunch tray without the food sliding off, and about finding my car after school. So, would you carry her tray for, say, the first six months? My car is a green Dodge, and there will be a dog waiting in it with me.

She has several special talents perhaps you should know about. For instance, she made up a cute little song about a bumble bee. If you ever could use it, I am sure her father would be delighted to come do the background buzzing. She can make French toast in her Easy-Bake oven, get to fifteen doing the lemon twist, and recently wrote a poem about "Giggley, the Wiggley Worm," which might be nice for the school paper.

If you will remember these few things about our Precious Angel, I am sure she will be your favorite student, destined to fame in the Red Robin Reading Group, the Talent Development Program, the Safety Patrol and, eventually, Phi Beta Kappa.

Should you need me, don't hesitate to call: 373-0689 (home); 332-5123 (office); 375-3969 (next door); 352-8197 (her dad's office); 382-1763 (the grocery store where I shop, just in case); 387-5211 (where Dad eats lunch); or 374-2221 (police).

I'll be happy to come sit in the desk with her, if you ever need me.

P.S. Please don't make her grow up too fast. We like her just the way she is!

WHEN GOD CREATED MOTHERS

ERMA BOMBECK
FROM *FOREVER, ERMA*

hen the good Lord was creating mothers, He was into His sixth day of overtime when the angel appeared and said, "You're doing a lot of fiddling around on this one."

The Lord said, "Have you read the specs on this order?

"She has to be completely washable, but not plastic;

"Have 180 movable parts...all replaceable;

"Run on black coffee and leftovers;

"Have a lap that disappears when she stands up;

"A kiss that can cure anything from a broken leg to a disappointed love affair;

"And six pairs of hands."

The angel shook her head slowly and said, "Six pairs of hands? No way."

"It's not the hands that are causing me problems," said the Lord. "It's the three pairs of eyes that mothers have to have."

"That's on the standard model?" asked the angel.

The Lord nodded. "One pair that sees through closed doors when she asks, 'What are you kids doing in there?' when she already knows. Another here in the back of her head that sees what she shouldn't but what she has to know, and of course the ones here in front that can look at a child when he goofs up and say, 'I understand and I love you,' without so much as uttering a word."

"Lord," said the angel, touching His sleeve gently, "come to bed. Tomorrow—"

"I can't," said the Lord. "I'm so close to creating something so close to myself. Already I have one who heals herself when she is sick…can feed a family of six on one pound of hamburger…and can get a nine-year-old to stand under a shower."

The angel circled the model of a mother very slowly and sighed. "It's too soft."

"But tough!" said the Lord excitedly. "You cannot imagine what this mother can do or endure."

"Can it think?"

"Not only think, but it can reason and compromise," said the Creator.

Finally the angel bent over and ran her finger across the cheek. "There's a leak," she pronounced. "I told you that you were trying to put too much into this model."

"It's not a leak," said the Lord. "It's a tear."

"What's it for?"

"It's for joy, sadness, disappointment, pain, loneliness and pride."

What do girls do who haven't any mothers
to help them through their troubles?
LOUISA MAY ALCOTT

JUST THE RIGHT SIZE

REV. MORRIS CHALFANT

It was the day before Mother's Day that a little boy, money tightly clutched in his hand, came to a department store to make a purchase. Bashfully he approached a woman clerk. "I want to buy a present for Mom." Then embarrassed, he added, "A slip."

"What size does she wear?"

He hesitated, "I don't know anything about sizes."

"Is she tall? Short? Large? Small?"

The lad was ready to answer. "Mother is just right!" He was so firm about it that the lady clerk wrapped up a size 36. The following Monday, the boy's mother returned to the store with the slip and exchanged it for a size 52! Size meant nothing to the lad; his mother had won his heart!

LETTING GO...

❧

LINDA ANDERSEN
FROM *DISCOVERY DIGEST*

*I*t was the in-between part of day—the delicious comma between afternoon and evening. Nature seemed to hold her breath, and day slid artlessly into envelopes of night. I surveyed the gentle hills framed in my window and basked in the bold orange of a day's end. A fluff of clouds embraced blazing edges of daylight in a farewell embrace. I was reminded of my daughter Dawn's cozy "goodbye" hug earlier. Being a mom had its moments.

I remember thinking, "I should be starting the meal. Maybe I should be using these few moments to improve my mind or job or write a letter— anything but watching a sunset." Wives don't have time to watch sunsets—do they? Well, this one was going to take time. It came only once a day and would be gone soon enough—like my daughter.

It was the in-between part of life for Dawn and me, too. She was 18, and all woman, all child. The mother in me wondered if all daughters were so much like the effervescent, fleeting sunshine of treasured sunsets. She was a little bit like magic: Now you see her, now you don't.

Shifting patterns of gold dusted the blood-red cloud patches over our fields as day sang its way into night. Each minute painted a new picture of bold strokes of color. It was like that with Dawn and me. Changing.

Always changing. A daughter perched on the edge of a nest, flapping her wings.

I didn't want the picture to change. I wanted almost desperately to preserve every nuance of color and shape so expertly painted on the canvas outside my window. I wanted to gild it in gold and tuck it in a private hiding place known only to me. Then I could take it out and enjoy it again at will.

Orange shafts of sun continued to melt into pots of gold and delicate mauve and finally to a shell pink before saying goodbye. It was over. A strange lump hung in my throat. The sunset was gone!

I remember sighing and turning reluctantly to the uneasy thoughts razoring their way into my mind. As Dawn left that day, my words floated behind her: "You will be home for dinner!" She had returned firmly, "I most likely will *not* be home for dinner." The air between us was taut. She was pulling away again. It had hurt, like taking off a new bandage. And it wasn't the first time. It would not be the last.

Still caught in the breathless beauty of a purple early evening, I recalled a scene long forgotten. I was a young mother, sitting in a first-grade classroom watching Dawn recite a finger-play game amid a circle of wide-eyed children. Her child eyes sparkled and caught mine over and over to make sure I was watching. Her lips had spread in a wide, warm grin that wrapped all the way around us both.

Once more, memory replayed an incident almost forgotten. "Mommy and Daddy" were leaving the house *without* Dawn. She was two, and her head reached just above the windowsill. Large tears rolled unheeded down red cheeks. She always wanted to go along. The parents had pulled away, impatient with the stage she was in, not realizing they would look back with longing.

A final memory flashed. Dawn as a young teen. Leaving. Always leaving. "Hello, Mom. See you later, Mom." Pulling away. It had begun. It would not turn back. Quite suddenly I realized that if I would ultimately keep my daughter, I must let go.

By this time, curtains of night were being drawn by an invisible hand over the horizon, announcing the end of this day and the anticipation of another. I can see myself, tracing the edge of the windowsill with my finger, and discovering a firm resolve growing inside to loosen the ties between us.

Dawn smiled from her picture on the mantel. I smiled back, shaking my head. Then, I had spoken aloud to the picture, as if to firm my resolve. "No more tug of war, kiddo. I can no more keep you than I can kidnap a sunset.

"You and sunsets are both strangely beautiful and strangely remote. Sometimes you are unreachable, and again you are warm and touchable… elusive as a runaway moonbeam. Are you both just for a time? Are you made to enjoy and dream over…and then let go? If so, then go ahead. It's the way of things. Wing your way, my pet. Perhaps the letting go will be the final bonding. You, like the sunset, will return in another form, at another time, in the right time…after you have tasted your freedom and tried your wings."

And she did. And it was ever so good.

Dear God,

I didn't think orange went with purple until I saw the sunset you made on Tuesday.

MARGARET
FROM *KIDS' LETTERS TO GOD*

MY SON'S PRESENT

DaLinda Blevins

My husband, Troy, and I took our two kids Christmas shopping last year. We were shopping for Dylan, Troy's nephew. My daughter, Da Cylla, was eleven and my son, Klintt, was six. So of course they already knew what Dylan "needed." Dylan had just turned a year old.

We walked down the toy aisle and tried to decide what to buy for a child who had everything. We looked at blocks and puzzles. Nothing caught my eye except the Mister Potato Head. I took the box from the shelf and read the little age appropriate sign at the bottom and Dylan was not old enough to have it. I told my husband and my kids that it was too bad because I had always wanted one when I was little and had never gotten one. As a matter of fact, I couldn't remember even seeing one outside of the box.

Dylan ended up getting the blocks.

A couple of days later we were sorting the presents under the tree.

Da Cylla and Klintt were counting how many each had. Klintt was very upset when he noticed I didn't have any. He didn't know that some weren't wrapped yet and the others were getting sized.

The next afternoon Troy took them to the same store to buy me a gift.

Klintt came home elated. But he didn't say a word. He kept the secret for another two weeks until Christmas morning.

Klintt insisted I open his first. I opened the neatly wrapped package to find my Mister Potato Head! My son's eyes were beaming with pride. "It's what you always wanted, Mommy."

THE BLESSING

It is true that there were times in the past when I would have or maybe did mumble the old curse, "May you have children like you." It turns out that I can still say the same words, but now they have turned into a blessing. "May you have children like you."

RICHARD ISRAEL
FROM *FOUR LETTERS TO MY CHILD*

Bedtime

After putting her children to bed, a mother changed into old slacks and a droopy blouse and proceeded to wash her hair. As she heard the children getting more and more rambunctious, her patience grew thin. At last she threw a towel around her head and stormed into their room, putting them back to bed with stern warnings. As she left the room, she heard her three-year-old say with a trembling voice, "Who was that?"

AUTHOR UNKNOWN

I WAS CHOSEN

SUSAN ALEXANDER YATES AND ALLISON YATES GASKINS
FROM *THANKS, MOM, FOR EVERYTHING*

t was time for bed and I really didn't mind too much. It meant Mommy would smooth my sheets and crawl in my bed with me. I'd snuggle in her arms and she'd rub my hair and tell me how special I was and how much she loved me. If it wasn't too late and Mommy wasn't too tired I might get to hear The Story before we said our prayers together.

I never grew tired of hearing her tell The Story. It was so special because it was about me. I was an only child and I was adopted. Mommy would begin by saying, "Your Daddy and I always wanted a baby. We wanted one for so long, and we kept praying that I would get pregnant and have a baby. But after several years when I didn't get pregnant, we began to realize that God had something even better for us. He decided that he was going to give us a very special baby—a baby that another lady was not able to take care of. He wanted parents who would be just right for this very special baby. Guess who that very special baby was! You!"

"Mommy, tell me about the day you got me."

"Well, Tucker," she would continue, "That was the most exciting day in my life! It began when the telephone rang, and a voice on the other end said, 'Mrs. Freeman, your beautiful little baby girl has just been born. Would you like to come see her?'

"I called your daddy at the office and he raced home and got me and we hurried to the hospital. At first we stood outside the window where all the new babies were and just looked at them, trying to figure out which one was you! When we got to the end of the row of babies, there you were and you turned your head and looked at us and seemed to smile!

"We couldn't wait to take you home and introduce you to our family and friends. When we drove up in front of our house, there were lots of friends who had come to see you and to bring you presents! You have always been such a gift to us. Why, the smartest thing Daddy and I ever did in our lives was adopt you!"

Each time Mother told me The Story she got excited. She never tired of telling it, and I never got tired of hearing her tell it. From the beginning she made me feel that being adopted was tremendously special, that I had somehow been chosen.

When I was about seven months pregnant with my own child, my mother came to visit. It was one of those really uncomfortable days, and the baby was kicking non-stop. As I groaned and held my stomach, my mother said, "It must be amazing to feel her kick."

Suddenly, it dawned on me that my mother had never felt a baby inside her womb.

"Mother," I said, "come and put your hands on my stomach. I want you to feel your grandchild."

The look of awe on my mother's face as she felt her granddaughter kick in the womb was so precious for me. I realized that I was able to give my mother a gift she had not been able to experience personally. She had given me so many gifts and finally I was able to share a very personal one with her.

TAKING PICTURES
WITH MY HEART

VICKEY L. BANKS

t was an extraordinary moment at the end of an otherwise ordinary
day.

I was walking down the hallway of our home when I came upon the
sweetest sight I had ever seen: my three-year-old son brushing his teeth.
No, it wasn't the fact that Parker *was* brushing his teeth; it was what he
looked like at that moment. With the aid of his well-used footstool, he still
had to stand on his tippy toes to barely see into the mirror. Clad only in
his tiny white T-shirt and "big boy" underwear, the little muscles in his
calves were clearly outlined. He looked so small, so innocent and pure.

I froze in place. Looking on, I realized that someday that same precious little boy would probably be bigger than I was. *He* would be able to
pick *me* up! So, I willed time to stand still for a few marvelous moments
while I soaked up the memory of what he looked like up on his tiptoes.

I thought of going to get my camera to capture the moment forever,
but I couldn't bear to turn away. Instead, I did what mothers have been
doing for centuries. I took a picture with my heart.

A Mother's Prayer

Lord,

When they scribble on the walls, please help me to see a rainbow!

And when I've said something a hundred times, please give me the patience to say it a hundred times more!

And on those particularly annoying days when I tell them to act their age, please help me to remember that they are!

And while we're on the subject of age, Lord, when I begin to lose my temper, please help me to remember to act mine!

And through it all, Lord—the fingerprints and runny noses, messy rooms and unrolled toilet paper, destroyed videotapes and broken knick-knacks—please help me to remember this:

Someday, these will be the days I will long to have back again!

ANGELA THOLE
FROM WHAT EVERY CHILD NEEDS

THE CATCHER NEST

RUTH SENTER
FROM *POWER FOR LIVING*

Sooner or later every parent faces the high school graduation of his first child. I am there and I am not sure I am prepared.

Unexpectedly, I receive a lesson in relinquishment today as we drive through the huge red-and-white sandstone rock masses that rise out of nowhere on the eastern slope of the Rocky Mountains.

I first notice the nest as we round the bend at the base of one of the giant stone walls. The hemisphere of sticks appears to be balanced on air, attached to the rock by invisible thread. I crane my neck to look upward and wish for my binoculars.

"That nest is at least 100 years old," my host tells me. "Lots of young eaglets have come and gone through that one. I'm told that the sticks used to build the nest would fill the back of a pickup truck."

I take mental inventory on my knowledge of eagles. I know they mate for life. Mother and father take turns sitting on the eggs and caring for the young. But my inventory does not include catcher nests.

"See that smaller nest below the big one?" my host asks. "That's called a catcher nest. When the eaglets are pushed out of the nest at about 12 weeks of age, their wings are not always strong enough for the distance. Mama and papa eagle build the catcher nest just in case their young one starts to fall. It's time to leave the nest but reinforcement is not far below."

I am silenced by the profound way of the eagle. My host has no idea of the impact his description has made on me.

Reinforcement. Yes, that's it! Divine reinforcement. The time has come for our Jori to leave the nest. I cannot block her need to fly any more than I can stop the calendar from moving toward graduation day.

Are her wings strong enough? I pray so. I have done my best to see that they are. But, when all is said and done, I do not know for sure.

But there is the "catcher nest"—God's reinforcement for the long haul. I am calmed by the catcher nest. Graduation day will come and go. The first day of college will come and go. Our home will no longer be where Jori lives.

But God is preparing reinforcement—His catcher nest—for her maiden voyage into life.

COLORS

I didn't know if my granddaughter had learned her colors yet, so I decided to test her. I would point out something and ask what color it was. She would tell me, and always she was correct. But it was fun for me, so I continued. At last she headed for the door, saying sagely, "Grandma, I think you should try to figure out some of these yourself!"

AUTHOR UNKNOWN

She Held His Hand

She held his hand when he was born
one sunlit April day.
She held his hand first day of school
then bravely drove away.

She held his hand and battled fears
above and under bed.
She held his hand then gave a kiss
before her son was wed.

She held his hand as on he bragged
through newborn daughter's cry.
She held his hand as his girl waved
when graduates passed by.

Yet it was he who held her hand
and watched her soul depart.
Though he no longer holds her hand
he holds her in his heart.

CARLA MUIR

Memories

THE GOOD TIMES

From now on, I am going to grab the good times with both arms. I am going to walk outside and feel the sun on my face and learn to laugh, really laugh again. Most of all, I'm going to take the love that comes my way and hold on to it for dear life. Sometimes we don't need new scenery, just new eyes.

DAWN MILLER
FROM *THE JOURNAL OF CALLIE WADE*

REMEMBERING

MAX LUCADO
FROM *THE INSPIRATIONAL STUDY BIBLE*

*I*f you've ever been a part of the following scene, you know you'll never forget it.

Inside the house is a quiet bedroom. Last spring's prom photo sits on the bedside table. A dried homecoming mum hangs from the bulletin board. Outside the house is a packed car. Both trunk and seat are full of clothes, books, and stereo. What was in the room is now in the car. The one who used to live in the room is about to drive the car…to college.

Both parent and child are stunned by the moment. What happened to childhood? Who fast-forwarded the years? Why, just yesterday this child was filling the house with cartwheels and playdough—now look. He's so tall. She's such a beauty. The child is grown.

The grown child is equally stunned. The road ahead looks lonely and long. There is safety in these walls. Protection. Security. Those pleas for independence so recently voiced are unheard today. "Just say the word, Dad, I'll stay. Just ask me, Mom, I won't leave."

But Mom and Dad know better. They know that love releases the loved. They know the training is over. The last bell has rung. The class is dismissed, and the application has begun.

And so parents and child hesitate at the side of the car. There's no time to teach new truths. There's no time to instill values or lay foundations. There is only one word that can be said—*remember.* Remember who loves you. Remember what matters. Remember what is right and what is wrong.

Remember.

KEEPSAKES

I love the word keepsake. *It is the opposite of overlooked, discarded, and forgotten. Special moments find their way into the treasure chest of our memories and become keepsakes of the heart.*

ALICE GRAY
FROM *KEEPSAKES OF THE HEART*

MY GRANDMOTHER'S SHELL

FAITH ANDREWS BEDFORD
FROM *THE QUIET CENTER*

*A*bove my mantel is a painting of a little girl with a conch shell. As she holds it up to the light, the sun streams through, turning the smooth, inner surface into glowing pink satin. No matter what the season, the painting's sunlight fills my study with summer's brightness.

Looking at the painting, I remember the story of its creation. The little girl is posing for her father, a painter. Her arms grow heavy, her neck aches, she longs to rest a bit. "El, El, look into the shell," her father murmurs, and she remembers what a privilege it is to pose for him, how sought-after his paintings are. "Just a bit longer," he promises, "and then we'll stop for tea."

Eleanor was my grandmother, and the painting—one that her father could not bear to part with—has been handed down through the generations. For as long as I can remember, the shell in the painting sat on my grandmother's desk. In the winter, when cold fog rolled in off the sea, she would hold it up to the lamp and its rosy sheen would fill her with summer's warmth again.

Grandmother found it washed up on the rocky shore of the little island in Maine that was her family's summer home. She used to tell me how, when the morning's silvery mist had lifted, she and her sisters and brother would run across the open meadows with their kites or pick bouquets of wildflowers or gather the wool left behind on the bushes by the wild island sheep. The children would hunt for blackberries and watch birds with their father, who taught them the birds' names and all their many songs. After tea, they often explored the wide beaches looking for pirate treasure. It was on one of these adventures that Grandmother found the shell, scoured smooth by the waves, bleached clean by the summer sun. As generations before her had done, she placed the shell to her ear and heard the sound of the sea.

By the time my mother was born, Grandmother had left that island home and created a new summer place for her own children. They spent hours sailing in little dinghies, galloping their ponies across the marshes, and gathering shells on the broad white beach that bordered Cape Cod Bay. In this new home Grandmother re-created many of her childhood loves: She seeded meadows with wildflowers, designed perennial borders, and planted blackberries. And from the porch she could look out across the tidal river and see ospreys nesting in a tall pine tree.

When we grandchildren began arriving, she set aside a part of her garden so we could know the joy of planting vegetables and flowers. How proud we were to place a plate of our radish harvest—ruby globes scrubbed shiny and clean—on a dinner table made brighter still by vases filled with our flowers. She taught us the birds' calls and told us how they returned each summer to her woods and meadows, just as we did. And she let us listen to the ocean in her shell.

Each autumn, as my family and I returned to our Midwestern home, I ached for the sounds of the shore: the cry of the gulls wheeling overhead, the low mournful song of the foghorn, so deep I seemed to feel more than hear it. The tangy smell of the salt air was replaced by the smoke of burning leaves. But I missed the tides and the wildness. Grandmother knew my yearning.

One year shortly after Thanksgiving, the postman brought a large box mailed from Massachusetts. Mother hid it in that secret place she kept all boxes that arrived in December. On Christmas morning I opened my grandmother's present and saw, nestled in tissue paper, the delicate pink and white of her shell. I picked it up and held it to my ear, and there was the ocean, murmuring. Outside, snow was falling softly past the window, but in the shell, cupped in my hand, waves lapped on a summer shore.

This year I have a granddaughter of my own. Her birth heralds the beginning of a new generation. When she comes to visit, I shall hold the shell up to her ear and she will hear the sound that has always drawn the women of our family to the ocean. It is the sound of her own heart.

You will find, as you look back upon your life, that the moments when you have really lived are the moments when you have done things in the spirit of love.

HENRY DRUMMOND

THE TABLE

JOHN V.A. WEAVER

N o, it isn't much of a table to look at. Just on old yellow oak thing,
I suppose you'd call it. It isn't that we couldn't have had mahogany
or walnut, of course. Only—well, thirty-eight years sort of turns anything
into a treasure.

It was Sam's father's wedding present to us. It and the six chairs—four
plain-bottomed, two with leather seats.

I recollect as well as yesterday the first supper we ate at it. We came
back from our honeymoon in Canada on a Monday afternoon. Sam had
made the lease for the little five-room house on Locust Street the week
before we got married.

All the month we were up there lazying around and fishing and getting used to each other I was worried about what we were going to do for
furnishing the dining room. I had a good deal of furniture from Mother's
house, and Sam had some from his flat, but neither of us had a dining
room table. We had talked a lot about it. But that trouble was settled the
minute we went into the room and saw the yellow oak, bright and shiny,
with a note from Father Graham on it.

I scrambled around and got some sort of a meal together. What it was
doesn't matter.

Pretty soon we were sitting in the chairs opposite each other, so close we could touch hands.

Sam didn't pay much attention to the food.

He kept looking at me. You know the way newlyweds will go on. Sam didn't say anything for a minute. Then he looked at me, and said, "I guess you're about the prettiest girl anywhere, Mary. I'm glad this table is so short. It lets me see you all the better."

I had to laugh. "Why, silly," I answered, "it opens in the middle. There's extra leaves in the china closet. We can make it as long as we want!"

He looked a little sheepish, and glanced around at the four other chairs. Then he grinned.

"Well," he said, "we'll have to use those leaves before we get through, I reckon."

I couldn't half eat for laughing. Yes, and blushing, too.

See that whole row of round dents up next to my place? That's what Sallie did with her spoon. She was the only one that always hammered. She was the first.

Over there, right by the opening—that's where Sam Jr. tried to carve his initials one time when he was about five. Sam caught him just as he was finishing the "S." It was a warm night for one young man, I can tell you.

Of course we'd put in one of the extra leaves a good many times before Ben came. The children were forever having friends over. Ben made the extra leaf permanent.

Then we commenced adding the second leaf. More friends, you see. Sam kept moving farther away from me, I used to tell him. He'd always answer the same thing. "My eyesight's all right," he'd say. "I can see just as well how pretty you are." And he said it as if he meant it.

So the children grew up and the table came to its longest. Sallie married Tom Thorpe when she was nineteen, and they both lived with us for three years.

The boys were in high school then, and I tell you we made a big family. All three extra leaves hardly did. Sam at one end and me at the other, Ben and Sam Jr. and Sallie and Tom—and my first granddaughter, Irene, in her high chair.

But she had her place, too. By that time we were in the big house on Maple, and the noise—and the life—and the happiness! The table was certainly getting battle-scarred. Look at that brown burnt place. That's where Senator Berkeley put down his cigar the night he stopped with us.

Well, then, Sam Jr. went off to college, and a little while after that Tom and Sallie set up housekeeping in their own home up on the Heights. So one of the leaves came out for good, and we didn't have so much use for the second, except for company once in a while. Except vacations, of course.

It was quite a shock when Sam Jr. left college at the end of his third year, and went out west to California. He didn't run off, you understand. We said he could go, although we were very disappointed he didn't stay and finish his education. But he was right. He's made a heap of money in real estate out there.

He comes back once a year for a week or so with Myra, that's his wife, and their two youngsters. Then the old table gets swollen back to its biggest. It seems mighty quiet when they go.

Ben came back and stayed with us two years after he graduated. We hoped he'd be content to settle down in town here for good, he was doing so well in life insurance. But that was just the trouble. The New York office wanted him, at twice the money, so he went. And the last leaf went out of the table with him.

That's been a year now. Sometimes I think of taking a roomer. Not just any ragtag and bobtail; some nice young fellow who needs a good home. It's so quiet—

I said so to Sam the other night. "My goodness," I said, "the table's so little again. Why, you're right on top of me. You can see all my wrinkles."

Sam laughed, and then he put his hand out and squeezed mine. "My eyes have grown dim to correspond," he answered. "You look as beautiful to me as ever. I guess you're about the prettiest girl anywhere."

But, still…

PINK SOCKS AND JEWELRY BOXES

ALLISON HARMS

This morning, my husband and I lingered over our morning ritual of coffee and cribbage.

Emma, our almost two-and-a-half-year-old daughter, already dressed in a scarlet tank top and denim skort, finished her pancake first. I wiped her hands and face while David removed her bib and highchair tray. The two of us sat down again while Emma trotted off to retrieve her tennis shoes from the laundry room.

When she returned with the shoes, I said, "What a big girl you are, sweetie, getting dressed all by yourself." I still felt amazed by her interest in choosing her own clothes and her ability to dress herself. Both had recently developed as significant modes of her self-expression. "Now, could you go to your room and get a pair of socks, please?"

"I will!" she said cheerfully and trotted off again. In a moment she came back with the socks, a pair of pink ones.

"Good choice, Emma!" I said. She twirled around the breakfast table, dancing with her happiness and her socks. She delighted in our attention and showing off the outfit she had picked out and put on herself. I lifted her onto my lap and began helping her put on the pink socks.

My husband winced. I knew Emma's color combination—pink, blue, and scarlet, with a lime green hair clip—was throwing him off. "Are you going to let her wear that?" David asked incredulously.

I smiled. "Are you going to let her build jewelry boxes out of two-by-sixes?"

We laughed together, remembering the story.

When David was about eight years old, he discovered some leftover pieces of wood in the garage. They were right triangle cut from the flight of basement stairs Dad had recently placed. David found these neatly-shaped blocks of wood irresistible; he was seized by the creative urge to build. He decided, on his own, to build a jewelry box for Mom.

He still remembers being completely absorbed in building that jewelry box. Level, square and firm—those were the rules of woodworking David had learned by watching Dad repair furniture, fix the fence, and construct the stairs. So David made a work of art and love that was level, square and firm—according to an eight-year-old using rough two-by-sixes. He enjoyed the physical creating of a gift he was proud to offer. It expressed himself and his love to Mom.

Looking back, David describes that gift as "more like a wooden tank, like a Tonka truck with a snowplow" rather than a jewelry box. He says it was hardly a box at all, but almost a solid block of wood, and very heavy. "My parents never let me know how ugly it was," David said. Instead, they treasured the jewelry box and encouraged his creative ideas. Dad started keeping a bin of leftover wood scraps in the garage and showed David and his brothers how to use his tools. He invited them to build whatever they could dream up. Mom affectionately displayed the jewelry box for years. David's overzealous hammer had bent the three-and-a-half-inch sixteen-penny nails in every direction so Mom had to keep the jewelry box on a doily to keep it from scratching her dresser, the first new piece of furniture she had ever purchased.

Eventually the jewelry box was retired to the attic with the other family heirlooms; David thinks his parents have left it to him in their will. Someday, David's daughter Emma will hold that jewelry box in her hands. She'll see how messy creativity can be, how awkward a child's attempts at expressing himself and his love are when viewed with grown-up eyes. But then she'll hear the story. And I hope she'll relate to how her own parents have encouraged her to express the gift of herself and understand how much we treasure those offerings.

But for now, Dave reached to tie Emma's shoelaces. "Okay," he said. "So much for controlling creative self-expression." Then he looked up and winked. "Got a doily?"

Happiness sneaks in through a door you didn't know you left open.

John Barrymore

SNOWSTORM IN TEXAS

LUCI SWINDOLL
FROM *WIDE MY WORLD, NARROW MY BED*

Since childhood I have always had somewhat of a flair for theatrics. My family was extremely demonstrative and outgoing, and we entertained each other with our crazy antics. I suppose when there is no television in one's home, families are inclined to create their own floor shows. We certainly did that...all the time. But, being the "ham" that I was, I gained enough confidence in-house to take my performances elsewhere. That was a mistake!

I must have been seven or eight years old and was walking home from school one hot afternoon, carrying an armload of books, when I became bored with this daily routine. So I decided to act as though I were in a violent snowstorm, actually battling for my life. For some reason I went all out! What were once school books became a shield to protect my face from the sudden, unexpected blizzard. I held them in front of me as I staggered about, falling once or twice, all the while making howling wind noises with my mouth. For a full minute or so it seemed realistic, but at the height of this production, when I looked up to see how far I was from shelter, the corner of my eye caught a view of the neighbor's porch. Every member of the family was there, sitting in utter silence staring at me, trying to comprehend what on earth had overcome the girl next door.

I found myself wishing the ground would open and swallow me up, but it didn't. Just as their laughter broke the silence, fear gripped my senses. To say I was mortified would have been an understatement. I ducked my head and raced home. It was literally weeks before I wanted to appear in public again, and once more the ritual of walking home from school returned to all accepted standards of conformity. Never again was there a snowstorm on a hot afternoon in Texas.

Several years after that embarrassing episode, my parents enrolled me in private elocution lessons with a fine teacher in Houston who had had an active, successful career on the New York stage. I loved those classes and benefited from them greatly, I'm sure, even though initially Mother and Dad may have done it to save the family name.

I would say that by virtue of my heritage, a tremendous love of the arts was probably inevitable. As far back into my life as I can draw up images, I envision my maternal grandmother, a piano teacher for thirty-three years, playing for either her own personal enjoyment or as accompaniment to the singing of her children and grandchildren. Also, my grandfather as a young man played trumpet in a small orchestra, I have been told. Both participated, through the years, in many church and civic music programs in the Texas town in which they lived, and together they fostered the love of music in each of their children.

One of my aunts—my mother's younger sister—while an artist by talent and education, is also an excellent pianist, and my mother loved to sing, majoring in voice during her college days. We often sang duets in church, she a soprano and I a contralto, and occasionally my two brothers joined us for quartets: Chuck, a tenor, and Orville, bass.

I can even recall, in the mothballs of my memory, scenes of the three of us as very young children, standing in stair steps on a drugstore counter, singing to the proprietor and local constituency for free ice cream cones. The more verses we sang, the more scoops we got! I think my father imagined us as the undiscovered von Trapp family replacements. He was utterly delighted to pack us off on these jaunts, always receiving verbal praise for his talented and fearless offspring. We sang for anybody who would listen and, as I remember, were completely at ease before an audience. It was fun, and after all, the goal of a double or triple decker cone gave us the incentive to sing every verse we had memorized.

There is a time for everything,
and a season for every activity under heaven…
a time to weep and a time to laugh,
a time to mourn and a time to dance.
ECCLESIASTES 3:1, 3–4

SIMPLE TREASURES

GARNET HUNT WHITE

*M*other accepted my friends as they were and they loved her for it. They liked the way she listened to their troubles and the clear advice she gave to them without preaching.

She made treasures out of simple things, be it clothes, crafts, or cooking.

An incident happened when I was twelve years old that made me appreciate Mother more. Up until that time, I had accepted her without realizing how important she was to me.

Mabel, who was almost thirteen years old, had asked me to go wading in Bill's Creek with Olive, Irene, and Esther. We twelve-year-old girls planned to take some snacks and picnic on the creek bank. However, I had forgotten to tell Mother about our plans for lunch.

All of us lived along Red Hill Dirt Road. My home was the last house before the creek. When the girls stopped for me, Mabel said, "Don't forget your cheese and crackers."

Hanging my head downward, I flushed. The blood pounded in my temples. I had forgotten to tell Mother about the food.

"Mother, can I have something to eat to take along?" I sheepishly asked.

"I don't have anything that's suitable for a picnic," Mother said. "You need food that's easy to handle."

"We've enough cheese and crackers for everyone," Mabel assured me, and we headed off for our afternoon adventure.

At the creek, Mabel laid the food on the sand at the water's edge.

We began wading and splashing in the cold, spring-fed stream. Although we held our skirts above our knees, the hems of our dresses were soon water soaked. The water's coldness on our feet and legs made our teeth chatter on that hot summer day.

My foot slipped off a rock; I tumbled into the icy water. Shivering and shaking from head to toe, I hurried to the sandbar to absorb some of the sun's warmth.

Soon the other girls began to chill and got out of the water to bask in the sun.

"Look!" Olive yelled. "Our lunch. The crackers are floating and the cheese is wet."

We hungry girls had no luck trying to eat the soggy crackers, but we chewed the cheese and shook in silence.

Then there was a soft noise behind us, and we turned. It was Mother!

"I thought you girls would be hungry by this time," she said. "I brought you a basket of food."

Mother handed each of us two warm biscuits filled with bacon, lettuce, and tomato. Mother had a biscuit sandwich with us, but she didn't gobble hers like we did.

"I'll bet the president isn't eating this good," Esther said.

"Mrs. Hunt, this is the most delicious food," Irene said to Mother.

"These biscuits are so good," Olive declared, "I could eat a dozen of them!"

"You knew we would be as hungry as hounds," Mabel said.

"Garnet," Irene said as she smiled at me, "your Mother is a prize."

We all knew what it took to bring us such a treat. Mother had to build a fire in the cookstove to get the oven hot enough to cook the biscuits; and then she stood over that heat to fry bacon for us.

"Mrs. Hunt, what can we do for you?" Mabel asked. "I know! We'll stop by your house and wash the dishes."

"They're washed," Mother told her. "I cleaned up everything before I left."

Before long it was time to gather our picnic and go home. "We'll walk back with you, and I'll carry your basket," Olive said as she jumped to her feet and snatched up the basket in which Mother had carried her gift.

I saw for the first time that my friends rated Mother higher than I did. On that summer afternoon, they made me realize how precious she really was.

Years later, when we had an all-electric home, I thought about Mother standing over that hot stove, frying bacon on a summer afternoon and waiting for the biscuits to brown. I truly wonder if I appreciated all the hardships Mother went through for me during my childhood.

When I think back over the sweet memories, I know why she is a treasure of my heart.

MY MOM'S AN R.N.

MARILYN MARTYN MCAULEY

*T*have always been proud that Mom was an R.N. and my childhood friends knew it all too well. If I wanted to add weight to my statement about some dread disease, I would remind them that my mom was an R.N. What more could they say?

It wasn't enough to say she was a nurse. I was well-informed about the levels of nursing. In the forties there was the P.N. and the R.N. Mom never told me these things. I learned by osmosis as I played within earshot of her conversations with her nurse friends. I discovered that an R.N. had more education and therefore was paid more, though not nearly enough for their skill and effort.

Mom set high standards for herself and those who worked under her, but the patient was the beneficiary. She was competent, compassionate, and creative in her profession. I know for she nursed me back to health through the usual childhood diseases and traumas. Such experiences gave me absolute confidence in her knowledge and I took to heart everything she taught me about health and hygiene.

Only once did I think she had gone too far in preventing me from getting sick. It was during World War II and Dad was fighting in the South Pacific. I was in the second grade when I brought a note home from the teacher saying our class had been exposed to chicken pox. You would have thought the battle had shifted from the Pacific to our home. Immediately I was told to strip for a bath. I watched with concern as she filled the tub with hot water. It was bad enough that steam was rising, but then she took the lid off the little brown bottle of disinfectant and poured a few drops in the water! She used this magic liquid on everything and now she was using it on me! I was terrified and began jumping up and down crying, "Mommy, Mommy, don't sterilize me!" Her method was pretty good though—I didn't get chicken pox until I was nine.

Mother subscribed to a nursing journal entitled R.N. One day, my neighbor friend was looking at the journal and asked me what R.N. meant. Mom and her friends always used the initials so I was left to my own imagination as to what they meant. With all of my eight-year-old wisdom I proudly informed my friend that it meant Real Nurse. It made sense to me. It's just as well I never gave thought to what P.N. stood for!

That evening, as I told Mom about the interchange I'd had with my friend, she began laughing. "You said what?"

"That R.N. meant Real Nurse."

That was when I learned that R.N. stands for Registered Nurse. Well, to my young mind, *registered* was not nearly as impressive as *real*. Though from third grade on I was more sophisticated in my knowledge and accurate in dispensing information, in my heart Mom remained my own real nurse...and the very best at that!

SISTER ROSALIE

PHILIP GULLEY
FROM *HOME TOWN TALES*

hen I was six, my mother went to work as a schoolteacher at a Catholic school in the next town over. The school sat next to the Catholic church. When the church was built, they hung a large fish symbol on the outside wall. For several years I thought my mother worked at a bait and tackle shop.

The other teachers were nuns. One of them was named Sister Rosalie, a hardy, humorous woman. She taught first grade. This was back in the days before mandatory kindergarten, so for many children Sister Rosalie was their first exposure to formal education. To this day, there are people in that town who sit up straight and clasp their hands when a nun enters the room.

The summer of my seventh year, my brother David underwent a hernia operation. Sister Rosalie came to baby-sit while my parents were at the hospital. The rest of us kids were deeply concerned, especially after my brother Glenn pointed out that David would get to recuperate on the couch for a solid week and pick the TV shows. Mistaking our worried expressions for sibling compassion, Sister Rosalie went to the kitchen to bake us a cake.

We were playing in the side yard when a muffled boom shook our house. We watched as the back screen door blew open and our cat streaked out, its fur blown off and whiskers singed. Sister Rosalie staggered out behind our cat, clutching her cross, her hosiery melted from her legs and hanging in shreds.

We had been having problems with our stove. The pilot light would go out. My mother would open the door, air out the room, then strike a match and relight the stove. Unfortunately, she forgot to relay that procedure to Sister Rosalie, and when the sister struck a match in a kitchen filled with gas, our stove was blasted to the heavens.

The year was 1968. Some people remember 1968 as the year of the Chicago riots and widespread national upheaval. The people of Martin Drive remember 1968 as the year a cake-baking nun almost blew our block to smithereens. We found our cat the next day huddled in a box, as disheveled as the war protesters in Chicago. We took her home, but she was never the same. Whenever nuns would come to visit, our cat would cower in a far corner and howl, tormented by feline flashbacks.

Several years after the explosion, Sister Rosalie left the classroom to become a hospital chaplain in the city. Now, when people in my Quaker meeting are sick, I visit them at the hospital where she ministers. On my way to their rooms, I stick my head in her office and holler "Boom!" Then I tell her coworkers all about 1968. I get the feeling Sister Rosalie wishes I'd take a job somewhere else.

Every year the nuns from the Catholic school hold a reunion at my parents' home. On their dining room wall hangs a family picture which was taken in 1968. Sister Rosalie looks at that picture, turns to my mother, and says, "That's how I remember your kids." I remember her standing on our back porch with singed hair and melted hosiery.

Next to my Grandma Norma, I think Sister Rosalie is the first saint I ever met. I've studied up on saints. Saints are people whose love for God causes them to do kind things even if they're dangerous. That pretty well describes baby-sitting.

Once when I was at the hospital, I saw Sister Rosalie comforting a patient, holding his hand and praying with him. I didn't yell "Boom!" then. I just stood and watched a saint in action and thought back to 1968 when all the world seemed crazy except for Grandma and Sister Rosalie.

My parents kept that stove another ten years. Forever after its broiler drawer hung askew, mute testimony to that turbulent year. Sister Rosalie, however, stood steady as an oak. That is what faith steeped in kindness can do.

Each moment of the year has its own beauty…a picture which was never seen before and which shall never be seen again.

RALPH WALDO EMERSON

A TEN-DOLLAR BILL

DON HAINES

When I was growing up my grandmother lived just a mile away. From the kitchen of her farmhouse she dispensed milk, cookies, advice, wisdom, and love. From her bank account every Christmas came a ten-dollar bill.

I was not the only one of her many grandchildren so favored. My grandmother distributed everything evenly, whether it was money or love. Every child felt special. No child ever felt left out.

Most people have memories of their grandmothers, and often one thing in particular will trigger those memories. For me it's a ten-dollar bill.

There was the time my first cousin and I played hooky from a chore my grandfather had assigned. We wandered off into the woods, right into a yellow jacket nest. Our grandfather wasted no sympathy on us. "You boys should've stayed in the bean patch" was his only comment. But my grandmother patiently applied baking soda paste to every bee sting while she dried our tears. "Boys do wrong things sometimes." She gave her little smile. "But these are still good boys." That's just one of the memories that comes back whenever I look at a ten-dollar bill.

My grandmother was a strong, quiet woman who ran a household where you always felt warm and safe. Nothing evil or ugly could ever penetrate the walls of Grandmother's house. Any grandchild with a problem was always welcome to come and talk it out. She'd sit quietly and listen to any tale of woe. Then, with a few well-chosen words, she'd lift the problem from weary young shoulders. I realize now she'd already experienced most of the problems she had to listen to. Maybe that's why her advice was even more valuable than her ten-dollar bills.

While helping others deal with their pain, she never spoke of her own. I found out from my mother that Grandmother's first child had died in infancy. Her second child and oldest daughter died at the age of twenty-one, just one week after her wedding day. One of her sisters committed suicide. Many people would have become embittered over such losses. Surely she hurt inside, but she never let it show. I can remember only a kind, gentle lady with a positive outlook. She gave love and security every day of her life. And every Christmas…a ten-dollar bill.

BACK HOME

EMMA STEWART
FROM *SEEK*

*A*s a child, I lived some distance back in the woods. The road wandered aimlessly like a writhing snake among huckleberry bushes and briers, along a sloping hillside where mountain laurel and honeysuckle blooms scented the air in late spring. It passed beside a field, which was enclosed with a barbed wire fence. Black Betty, our cow, was pastured there. Growing profusely beside the fence were large lavender violets.

When the road got tired of winding, and I got tired of walking, we were always at the same place. The huge boxwood bushes stood tall and graceful, as though they were soldiers, guarding a humble little shack, the closest place to heaven—my home.

There was a two-story frame dwelling, politely asking for a fresh coat of whitewash. It had a tin roof, painted as red as a strawberry, that rattled when the wind blew. A wisteria vine was tightly clinging to the front-porch columns, and a rusty screen door shrieked loudly when it was opened.

The floor was bare except for a few scatter rugs my grandma had crocheted with a button hook. The ceilings were high, and draped with a few cobwebs. The mantle was decorated by a seven-day alarm clock that had been on vacation for years. A kerosene lamp, its globe black from smoke, stood atop a dresser in the corner.

To the chimney was attached an old cast-iron heater, cracked down the side, which gave us comfortable warmth in cold weather. There was also a box of neatly sawed oak wood.

During the summer we waved a palm leaf fan to stir up a little breeze. However, the second floor was air-conditioned rather well by a "balm-o-gilead" tree that swayed with the wind and circulated a gentle breeze through our upstairs windows.

We ate in a little kitchen which stood out in the backyard away from the main house. The kitchen was like an icebox in the winter and a furnace in summer.

We had an ugly, old black cookstove, a huge square table covered usually with a bright floral-patterned oilcloth, and some round-back wooden chairs. A bucket of water from the moss-covered well in the back-yard was placed on a little table by the stove, and a coconut shell dipper hung beside the bucket. Electricity hadn't found its way to our part of the country yet.

But our food was good. Nothing can quite compare to the homemade biscuits, fried ham sizzling in red gravy, cabbage floating in ham grease, or butter cake with homemade chocolate icing. My mother would stand on the kitchen porch and call out when the meals were ready.

I spent a lot of time on the barrel-stave hammock in the backyard under the old gnarled trees. I would swing for hours in the fresh air and sunshine and become lost in pleasant reverie. That was my idea of recreation. I didn't know what it was to be lonely.

Mama was a delightful person. She was tall, stately and slender, with warm brown eyes. Her long black hair was tucked in a bun at the nape of her neck. She was always busy cooking, churning, feeding chickens, washing clothes on an old scrub board, or drawing water with a windlass and rope from a fifty-foot well. But she found time to rock and cuddle me, and sew for my dollies.

Daddy walked behind a mule and a horse and a double plow all day, turning up fresh ground and putting out of sight old dead grass and broom straw. There were fresh earthy smells everywhere. In the distance a crow would "caw," and Daddy would mock him and try to frighten him away.

After supper sometimes we'd walk out to a neighbor's house, or else we'd just sit and talk or play the hand-cranked Victrola. Life was simple for us, but it was good.

Since those days the world has changed a great deal—and so have I. With all our progress though, love is still the greatest force on earth. I saw it in my parents long ago. It was love that made a humble country home seem like heaven.

THE STITCHES THAT BIND

LINDA SUNSHINE
FROM *THE QUIET CENTER*

My grandmother believed that you could tell a lot about a woman from her needlework, especially if you looked on the wrong side. "You can't hide anything from the back," she would say. In many ways, the story of the women in my family can be told through our needlework.

Grandmother crocheted lace—tiny, white snowflake shapes—spun from fine cotton thread and sewn together into huge cloths. Each one took several years to complete. She was a stern, disciplined woman whose ramrod straight spine never quite touched the back of her chair. She believed in correct posture and high standards for herself and everyone else. There are no right or wrong sides to my grandmother's cloths. They are perfect, any way you look at them.

I have the lace cloth Grandmother made for my aunt, and, even after almost thirty years, her work has held firm. It was stitched together with such precision that it never needs mending. Like my grandmother, it refuses to unravel.

My mother, on the other hand, is much less stringent about her work. She enjoys the challenge of taking on seemingly impossible projects—wall-size needlework pictures (copied from the cover of the first book I ever published as a young editor) or huge sweater-coats knit on the smallest needles. She is now knitting a sweater so intricate that each row of stitches is different, and suede strips are woven into the wool. It will be a showcase piece, but, like all my mother's work, after a few wearings threads will hang out and holes will form where the pieces are not carefully woven together. The backs of my mother's sweaters are a creative jungle, I think, because my mother swallows time in huge gulps. She works furiously to complete a project and then get started on the next one. In her haste, she will not stop to tuck in loose threads.

My sister, certainly the most talented among us, creates her own designs and executes them in painstaking detail. She knows how to follow directions, and she does not believe in shortcuts. My mother and I defer to her whenever we're confused by a knitting pattern. She alone has the patience to reason out any instructions whatsoever, no matter how complicated they seem to us.

You will never find a flaw in a pillow or sweater my sister has completed. She is the only one in the family who will rip out an entire sleeve if she discovers so much as one slipped stitch in the cuff, even if you can see it only when the sweater is inside out. My mother and I tease her, but, at the same time, we know it is this very perfectionism that gives her work the kind of quality lacking in ours. It is no surprise my sister's crocheted pocketbooks have sold for hundreds of dollars in retail stores.

As for myself, I get impatient with directions. Being told what to do brings out a rebellious streak—I always think I can come up with an easier way to make something. Usually I'm wrong. I make lots of mistakes, and I tend to ignore them (assuming they will go unnoticed or, if not, most people will be too polite to say anything).

But, for all the sleeves that are not exactly the same length, the insides of my sweaters are nearly as meticulous as my sister's. Perhaps because of my grandmother, I value perfection; perhaps because of my mother, I have a weakness for believing in my own creativity. I work hard at finishing touches. Consequently the insides of my sweaters often look far better than the outsides.

When my nephew Adam was born, my mother, my sister, and I went into a frenzy of sweater making. Cardigans, pullovers, vests, jackets—if it could be made with knitting needles, the child had it. By the time he was five years old, Adam's hand-knit wardrobe could easily clothe his entire kindergarten class.

Stack those sweaters up and you'll have a barometer of the women in my family. They are tributes of our devotion, our love, and our mutual compulsion. Yes, those sweaters will tell you a lot about us, especially if they're turned inside out.

THE ROSE

Nancy I. Pamerleau

When I was a little pigtailed six-year-old I went to our old-time dime store, which was complete with squeaky wooden floor and the smell of popcorn and penny candy. I was in search of just the right Mother's Day gift. After carefully examining the items my small allowance could buy, I chose a plastic red rose. Smuggling it into my bedroom, I composed a poem for the special occasion and proudly presented the gift to my mother.

After her death, I found that rose, faded and dusty, but still proudly displayed in a crystal vase on a silver tray. Not until then did I realize how much it had meant to her. She had saved it for thirty years. The Christmas that followed her death was a time of grief. We missed the traditional family dinner she prepared, her lavish, color-coordinated Christmas table of green plates and red goblets, and her love of giving, especially to her grandchildren.

To console me, my husband bought several special gifts we really couldn't afford. After opening these, I still grieved. Then I saw the gift from my son.

"I picked it out myself, Mom," my six-year-old proudly announced, hand extended. I smiled broadly and felt great consolation as I accepted his treasure. An angel must have whispered in his ear as he made that choice. His gift was an artificial red rose.

THE CHRISTMAS NANDINA

ELIZABETH SILANCE BALLARD

Nandina: "Nan-deena" An evergreen shrub with red berries and used by the Norbert family as a tabletop "Christmas tree." Paul Norbert

Nandina: "Nan-deena" A very lovely evergreen bush with red berries. It should stay in the yard and is definitely NOT a Christmas tree. Anne Norbert

Anne and Paul had their first marital spat on December 15, three months after the wedding. Anne had been making exquisite lace ornaments for weeks and now she wanted to buy their first Christmas tree, a special tree, one they would always remember.

"But we already have our Christmas tree," Paul told her, and he went to the patio to get the nandina bush.

"A bush?" she asked, laughing, believing he must be teasing her. "A bush in a black plastic pot?"

But Paul was not teasing.

"The Norberts always have a nandina bush at Christmas. I guess I should have told you sooner but it never occurred to me because it's just something we've done since I was twelve years old. It's our holiday tradition now and I won't change it."

Her face flushed. Oh, the nandina bush was pretty in its own way. It had been out on their patio since the day after their wedding when Paul had moved his things from the apartment he shared with his two brothers. Pretty as it was, though, it was not a Christmas tree. It was not something she wanted to place her lovely handmade ornaments on and it would hardly hold even one string of the tiny white lights.

"But why?"

"Listen, Anne," he said. "Dad died when Davey was two years old and Mom did her best for the next three years. Then she got sick."

Anne listened as he went on to explain that his mother, Julia, had lost so many hours at the hosiery mill due to her illness that what little she had been able to provide for her three sons deteriorated rapidly. Mounting medical bills took priority as she tried desperately to get well.

"That was the first year we did not have a Christmas tree," Paul said, holding her close. "Randy was eight, Davey was five, and I was twelve—and disgusted. I wanted a Christmas tree. All my friends had one and I was angry that we couldn't have one, too.

"A week before Christmas Mom came home from her doctor's visit and told me she needed surgery and that she would be going into the hospital on December 26. She said she had been hoping to work extra hours but she hadn't been able to do so."

"I'm going to need your help, Paul, to make Christmas special this year," she had told her oldest son.

Resentfully, Paul had listened to his mother's idea and helped her dig up the nandina bush from the yard and put it in a black plastic pot.

"I've always loved nandinas," she had said. "My grandmother had nandinas in her yard back in North Carolina and there were always lovely red berries at Christmastime. See how many berries there are? They'll show up pretty if you and the boys put a few ornaments on it."

Paul thought of the tall trees with glittering ornaments and stars his friends had described, and the nandina bush seemed a poor substitute.

"We tried to decorate it to look like a real Christmas tree, and Randy and Davey thought it was great fun. Davey was too young to remember the Christmas trees we had in the past and Randy was always good-natured and eager to please so he didn't even question this strange substitute. No. I was the only one who hated the thing."

Julia had made it clear she understood Paul's anger and disappointment but she went on with her arrangements—packing a small bag for the hospital and trying to prepare food for them to have until she could get back home.

"On Christmas Eve morning we all walked the six blocks to church with us boys fussing when we had to stop several times to let Mom rest. When we finally reached the gray stone steps she told me to stay outside with my brothers until she came back."

After a while Paul began to get anxious. People were arriving for the special children's service and to see the living nativity on the church lawn.

"My brothers were restless and started arguing and I was worried that we would be late for the service. Besides, I was angry that I had been left outside with them so I went to find Mom."

Paul had wandered through the halls until he heard his mother's voice, talking softly and crying. It was something he had never seen his mother do.

"…and—well, if anything happens to me, my boys…"

Paul's heart pounded as he stood listening.

"My oldest one, Paul—well, he's had to help me so much since I've been sick. I really…"

"It wasn't until then that I knew Mom was much sicker than I had realized and that she was very worried about us. I slipped back outside and told the boys that I couldn't find her and when she came out she was smiling. Randy and Davey didn't even notice that her face was swollen and her eyes still teary and we all went inside to the children's Christmas Eve service as if nothing were wrong."

Paul had no idea when they were delivered, but the next morning there had been several gifts piled on the table by the nandina bush. One for each of them from Julia and the others from their friends at church.

"There were two gifts for me," Paul said, smiling at the memory. "A Scrabble game and a book—a Hardy Boys mystery. I still have them."

Julia had lain on the sofa all smiles as the little boys screeched in the delight of ripping the bright wrapping paper. She had made their favorite breakfast—hot chocolate and monkey bread.

"Later in the morning, Randy's Sunday school teacher brought a huge tray of turkey, dressing, and a bag of other good things we had not eaten for a very long time. After Randy and Davey went to bed that night, Mom gave me pen and paper and asked me to write a thank-you note to our church who had provided for us on such short notice when she had been unable to do so herself.

"Mom went to sleep lying on the sofa, watching the tiny lights twinkle on the nandina bush while I sat at the kitchen table rewriting the thank-you note she had dictated so that it would be neat as she insisted.

"The next day she went to the hospital and she never came home. That was the first Christmas 'tree' that Davey would remember and it was the last one we had with Mom. We came to North Carolina to live with Aunt Violet who loved us and helped us through that first lonely, frightening year. Most of all she understood why, the following Christmas, we insisted on decorating the nandina bush we had brought from home.

"I love you, Anne, but in this one thing I won't give in."

Anne nodded, unable to speak, now seeing beyond the simple little bush to the love of a mother long departed who had left three sons behind, each possessing her quiet strength and tenderness. Julia had bequeathed to them a legacy of love, which now included Anne, and would include the children of Paul and Anne who were yet to come; children with whom they would share each year the story of the Christmas nandina.

SILVER THREADS AND GOLDEN NEEDLES

FAITH ANDREWS BEDFORD
FROM *MARY ENGELBREIT'S HOME COMPANION*

*I*n the corner of my daughter's room is a little doll's bed covered with a tiny pink bedspread. The coverlet was my first sewing project, made from a snippet of a larger one Grandmother had sewn for herself.

As a little girl I felt Grandmother could make anything in the world. If I admired a blouse in a magazine, its twin would appear the next week. My dolls had wardrobes fit for a princess.

To a child, Grandmother's sewing box was a magic treasure chest: neat rows of brightly colored spools, scrollwork scissors in a tiny red leather case, glass-headed pins bristling on a red cloth tomato. Best of all was the button box. There were sparkling rhinestone squares, blue wooden flower buttons, engraved pewter hearts and lots of mother-of-pearl buttons cut from shirts too worn to be rescued. Grandmother wasted nothing.

In the fifties, Home Economics was required for all girls. The sewing room had neat rows of shiny black sewing machines with drawers full of mysterious metal contraptions. We learned to wind a bobbin, make a flat-felled seam and master that most difficult of tasks—putting in a zipper.

Moving from pot holders through aprons to gathered skirts, we planned the spring fashion show. As I walked down the runway in my red calico shirtwaist, I saw Grandmother's proud face and smiled. Only she knew I'd ripped out the zipper three times.

When my parents gave me a clothing allowance, I realized I could buy one skirt or make three. The beautiful prom dresses in *Seventeen* could be re-created once Grandmother showed me how to adapt patterns. I graduated from *Simplicity* patterns to *Vogue*. But in racing to complete an outfit, I frequently made mistakes. One afternoon, finding me in tears over a totally ruined corduroy jumper, Grandmother encouraged me to master the discipline of finishing just one step or two at a time. The careful progression from cutting and marking to finishing created an orderly pattern in my teenage life. Concentrating on the precise intricacies of fitting in a gusset distracted me from such adolescent anxieties as biology tests, boyfriends, or drama tryouts.

Prom dresses gave way to business suits and then a wedding dress. Grandmother helped me pack my home-sewn honeymoon wardrobe: a long skirt and ruffled blouse for fireside wearing at our ski lodge. For our new apartment, I slip-covered all our hand-me-down furniture.

When our first baby arrived, I learned to appliqué; little sailboats and trains decorated his sunsuits. The arrival of two daughters became an opportunity for embroidery and ruffles. During their naptimes, the quiet discipline of sewing became my own brand of therapy. I realized then, that my grandmother's gift to me has touched all realms of my life for she helped me see the fulfillment in creavtivity which has extended far beyond needle and thread.

Grandmother has been gone for many years now, but her gift to us continues. As my children have grown and wanted things they could not find or afford, they too have discovered the creative pleasures of sewing. Our rock-climbing son, recoiling from the expense of Lycra climbing pants, made his own. Our older daughter brought home thrift shop finds and altered them to become her own special creations. The youngest has learned the knack of combining pattern pieces to create unique garments.

Now I have grandchildren of my own. As I work on their dresses and jumpers, I realize these little garments are stitched together with the same thread Grandmother gave to me, the thread that binds generations together—the thread of love.

Life

❦

DYNAMO

She was old in years but young in spirit. Although she got around on crutches and in a wheelchair, she was a dynamo. She ran a highly successful real estate business, served on the town council, and regularly helped charitable causes in various capacities.

One day a new friend asked what had put her in the wheelchair.

"Infantile paralysis," she replied. "In the beginning, I was almost completely paralyzed."

"It's obviously still a serious disability," said the friend. "How do you cope, how do you do all the things you do?"

"Ah!" she said with a smile, "the paralysis never touched my heart or my head."

AUTHOR UNKNOWN
FROM MORE OF…THE BEST OF BITS & PIECES

MARGARET
AND HER PENNIES

PHILIP GULLEY
FROM *HOME TOWN TALES*

Every Monday morning, my friend Jim and I eat breakfast at Bob Evans' and swap war stories. Jim pastors an inner-city church, and his stories have more meat and gristle than mine.

One morning he told me about Margaret. Margaret is an eighty-year-old widow in his church. She lives in a retirement center and ventures out once a week to buy groceries at Safeway. Margaret, Jim reports, is a sweet lady, though that hasn't always been the case. She told Jim that when she was younger she was not a good person, but God has slowly changed her. Occasionally, God builds the house overnight, but most times God nails up one board each day. Margaret was a board each day.

Several years ago, Margaret felt God wanted her to do something for her inner-city church. So she prayed about it, and after a while the Lord told her to save all her pennies for the children of the church. Margaret was hoping for something a little grander, but she didn't complain. A person has to start somewhere, she told Jim. So every year at Christmas, she wrapped up her pennies, about ten dollars' worth, and gave them to her church. She told them it was for the kids and not to spend it on pew cushions.

One afternoon a lady down the hall from Margaret came to visit. She noticed Margaret's mayonnaise jar full of pennies. She asked her why she was saving pennies. Margaret told her it was for the kids at church.

"I don't have a church," the lady said. "Can I save up my pennies and give them to the kids in your church?"

"Suit yourself," Margaret said.

Before long, thirty folks in the retirement center were saving their pennies for the kids.

Every Wednesday, they climb on the retirement center's bus and drive to the Safeway. They steer their carts up and down the aisles, then stand in line at the checkout counter. They put their groceries on the moving belt and watch as each price pops up on the display. When the checker calls the total, the old folks count out the money a bill at a time. Then they ask for the change in pennies. They count that out, too, one penny at a time. The other customers stand behind them and roll their eyes. They don't know a work of God is underway.

The next year at Christmastime, the women loaded up their jars and took their pennies, twenty thousand of them, to the church Christmas party. The kids staggered from the Christmas party, their pockets bursting with pennies.

When the kids found out who was behind the pennies, they wanted to visit the retirement center and sing Christmas carols. Pastor Jim took them in Big Blue, the church bus. They assembled in the dining room. Jim watched from the back row. In front of him sat one of the retirement center ladies. Jim didn't know her, had never seen her. She was explaining to a visitor what was going on.

"These children, you see, they're from our church, and they've come to visit us. We're awfully close."

The next week, one of the men in the retirement center passed away. Jim came and conducted the memorial service right there at the retirement center, which is fast becoming the new church annex.

All of this, mind you, began with Margaret in her apartment praying to the Lord to let her do a mighty work. She admits now that she was a little disappointed when God told her to save her pennies. She was hoping for a more flamboyant ministry. She didn't want to start with pennies.

Then she thought back on her own life and how sometimes God builds houses one board each day.

MORNING PRAYER

So far today, Lord, I've done okay. I haven't gossiped, haven't lost my temper, been greedy, grumpy, selfish or mean. I'm really glad about that.

But in a few minutes, Lord, I'm going to get out of bed, and from then on I'm going to need a lot of help. Amen.

A STORY TO LIVE BY

ANN WELLS
FROM *THE LOS ANGELES TIMES*

My brother-in-law opened the bottom drawer of my sister's bureau and lifted out a tissue-wrapped package. He discarded the tissue and handed me the slip. It was exquisite; silk, handmade and trimmed with a cobweb of lace. The price tag with an astronomical figure on it was still attached. "Jan bought this the first time we went to New York, at least 8 or 9 years ago. She never wore it. She was saving it for a special occasion. Well, I guess this is the occasion." He took the slip from me and put it on the bed with the other clothes we were taking to the mortician. His hands lingered on the soft material for a moment, then he slammed the drawer shut and turned to me. "Don't ever save anything for a special occasion. Every day you're alive is a special occasion."

I remembered those words through the funeral and the days that followed when I helped him and my niece attend to all the sad chores that follow an unexpected death. I thought about them on the plane returning to California from the Midwestern town where my sister's family lives. I thought about all the things that she hadn't seen or heard or done. I thought about the things that she had done without realizing that they were special.

I'm still thinking about his words, and they've changed my life. I'm reading more and dusting less. I'm sitting on the deck and admiring the view without fussing about the weeds in the garden. I'm spending more time with my family and friends and less time in committee meetings. Whenever possible, life should be a pattern of experience to savor, not endure. I'm trying to recognize these moments now and cherish them.

I'm not "saving" anything; we use our good china and crystal for every special event...such as losing a pound, getting the sink unstopped, the first camellia blossom.

I wear my good blazer to the market if I feel like it. My theory is if I look prosperous, I can shell out $28.49 for one small bag of groceries without wincing. I'm not saving my good perfume for special parties; clerks in hardware stores and tellers in banks have noses that function as well as my party-going friends'.

"Someday" and "one of these days" are losing their grip on my vocabulary. If it's worth seeing or hearing or doing, I want to see and hear and do it now. I'm not sure what my sister would have done had she known that she wouldn't be here for the tomorrow we all take for granted. I think she would have called family members and a few close friends. She might have called a few former friends to apologize and mend fences for past squabbles. I like to think she would have gone out for a Chinese dinner, her favorite food. I'm guessing...I'll never know.

It's those little things left undone that would make me angry if I knew that my hours were limited. Angry because I put off seeing good friends whom I was going to get in touch with...someday. Angry because I hadn't written certain letters that I intended to write...one of these days. Angry and sorry that I didn't tell my husband and daughter often enough how much I truly love them. I'm trying very hard not to put off, hold back, or save anything that would add laughter and luster to our lives.

And every morning when I open my eyes, I tell myself that it is special.

Every day, every minute, every breath truly is...a gift from God.

SUCH AS I HAVE

BONNIE SHEPHERD

ith only two weeks before Christmas, the last place I wanted to be was in the hospital recovering from surgery. This was our family's first Christmas in Minnesota, and I wanted it to be memorable, but not this way.

For weeks I had ignored the pain in my left side, but when it got worse, I saw the doctor. "Gallstones," he said, peering at the X rays. "Enough to string a necklace. You'll need surgery right away."

Despite my protests that this was a terrible time to be in the hospital, the gnawing pain in my side convinced me to go ahead with the surgery. My husband, Buster, assured me he could take care of things at home, and I called a few friends for help with carpooling. A thousand other things—Christmas baking, shopping, and decorating—would have to wait.

I struggled to open my eyes after sleeping for the better part of two days in the hospital following my surgery. As I became more alert, I looked around to what seemed like a Christmas floral shop. Red poinsettias and other bouquets crowded the windowsill. A stack of cards waited to be opened. On the stand next to my bed stood a small tree decorated with ornaments my children had made. The shelf over the sink held a dozen red roses from my parents in Indiana and a yule log with candles from our neighbor. I was overwhelmed by all the love and attention.

Maybe being in the hospital around Christmas isn't so bad after all, I thought. My husband said that friends had brought meals to the family and offered to look after our four children.

Outside my window, heavy snow was transforming our small town into a winter wonderland. The kids have to be loving this, I thought as I imagined them bundled in their snowsuits building a backyard snowman, or skating at Garfield School on the outdoor ice rink.

Would they include Adam, our handicapped son? I wondered. At five years old, he had just started walking independently, and I worried about him getting around on the ice and snow with his thin ankles. Would anyone take him for a sled ride at the school?

"More flowers!" The nurse's voice startled me from my thoughts as she came into the room carrying a beautiful centerpiece. She handed me the card while she made room for the bouquet among the poinsettias on the windowsill.

"I guess we're going to have to send you home," she teased. "We're out of space here!"

"Okay with me," I agreed.

"Oh, I almost forgot these!"

She took more cards from her pocket and put them on the tray. Before leaving the room, she pulled back the pale green privacy curtain between the two beds.

While I was reading my get-well cards, I heard, "Yep, I like those flowers."

I looked up to see the woman in the bed beside me push the curtain aside so she could see better. "Yep, I like your flowers," she repeated.

My roommate was a small forty-something woman with Down's syndrome. She had short, curly gray hair and brown eyes. Her hospital gown hung untied around her neck, and when she moved forward it exposed her bare back. I wanted to tie it for her, but I was still connected to an IV. She stared at my flowers with childlike wonder.

"I'm Bonnie," I told her. "What's your name?"

"Ginger," she said, rolling her eyes toward the ceiling and pressing her lips together after she spoke. "Doc's gonna fix my foot. I'm gonna have *suur-jeree* tomorrow."

Ginger and I talked until dinnertime. She told me about the group home where she lived and how she wanted to get back for her Christmas party. She never mentioned a family, and I didn't ask. Every few minutes she reminded me of her surgery scheduled for the next morning. "Doc's gonna fix my foot," she would say.

That evening I had several visitors, including my son Adam. Ginger chatted merrily to them, telling each about my pretty flowers. But mostly, she kept an eye on Adam. And, later after everyone left, Ginger repeated over and over, just as she had about my flowers, "Yep, I like your Adam."

The next morning Ginger left for surgery, and the nurse came to help me take a short walk down the hall. It felt good to be on my feet.

Soon I was back in our room. As I walked through the door, the stark contrast between the two sides of the room hit me. Ginger's bed stood neatly made, waiting for her return. But she had no cards, no flowers, and no visitors. My side bloomed with flowers, and the stack of get-well cards reminded me of just how much I was loved.

No one sent Ginger flowers or a card. In fact, no one had even called or visited.

Is this what it will be like for Adam one day? I wondered, then quickly put the thought from my mind.

I know, I decided. I'll give her something of mine.

I walked to the window and picked up the red-candled centerpiece with holly sprigs. But this would look great on our Christmas dinner table, I thought, as I set the piece back down. What about the poinsettias? Then I realized how much the deep red plants would brighten the entry of our turn-of-the-century home. And, of course, I can't give away Mom and Dad's roses, knowing we won't see them for Christmas this year, I thought.

The justifications kept coming: the flowers are beginning to wilt; this friend would be offended; I really could use this when I get home. I couldn't part with anything. Then I climbed back into my bed, placating my guilt with a decision to call the hospital gift shop when it opened in the morning and order Ginger some flowers of her own.

When Ginger returned from surgery, a candy-striper brought her a small green Christmas wreath with a red bow. She hung it on the bare white wall above Ginger's bed. That evening I had more visitors, and even though Ginger was recuperating from surgery, she greeted each one and proudly showed them her Christmas wreath.

After breakfast the next morning, the nurse returned to tell Ginger that she was going home. "The van from the group home is on its way to pick you up," she said.

I knew Ginger's short stay meant she would be home in time for her Christmas party. I was happy for her, but I felt my own personal guilt when I remembered the hospital gift shop would not open for two more hours.

Once more I looked around the room at my flowers. Can I part with any of these?

The nurse brought the wheelchair to Ginger's bedside. Ginger gathered her few personal belongings and pulled her coat from the hanger in the closet.

"I've really enjoyed getting to know you, Ginger," I told her. My words were sincere, but I felt guilty for not following through on my good intentions.

The nurse helped Ginger with her coat and into the wheelchair. Then she removed the small wreath from the nail on the wall and handed it to Ginger. They turned toward the door to leave when Ginger said, "Wait!"

Ginger stood up from her wheelchair and hobbled slowly to my bedside. She reached her right hand forward and gently laid the small wreath in my lap.

"Merry Christmas," she said. "You're a nice lady." Then she gave me a big hug.

"Thank you," I whispered.

I couldn't say anything more as she hobbled back to the chair and headed out the door.

I dropped my moist eyes to the small wreath in my hands. Ginger's only gift, I thought. And she gave it to me.

I looked toward her bed. Once again, her side of the room was bare and empty. But as I heard the "ping" of the elevator doors closing behind Ginger, I knew that she possessed much, much more than I.

I long to put the experience of fifty years at once into your young lives, to give you at once the key of that treasure chamber every gem of which has cost me tears and struggles and prayer, but you must work for these inward treasures yourselves.

HARRIET BEECHER STOWE

HOOKED ON CRAFTS

PATSY CLAIRMONT
FROM *NORMAL IS JUST A SETTING ON YOUR DRYER*

I do crafts. No, wait, that's not quite right. I *own* crafts. I have snarls of thread meant for needlepoint and gnarly-looking yarn for afghans. I have how-to books worn from my reading and rereading of the instructions. Swatches of material, florist wire, paint brushes, grapevines, and (every crafter's best friend) a hot glue gun—along with a myriad of additional stuff—greet me whenever I open my closet door.

Every time I'm enticed into purchasing a new project, I think, *I'll finish this one for sure.* I've attempted everything from oil painting, floral arranging, quilts, and scherenschnitte (German paper cutting) to quilling.

"Quilling?" This craft requires you to wind teeny strips of paper around the tip of a needle. Once they're wound, you glue the end with a toothpick applicator so your paper coil doesn't spring loose. With a pair of tweezers, you set your coil onto a pattern attached to a foam board, securing it with a straight pin. Then you start the paper-twirling process over again.

You may be wondering how many of those paper tidbits one needs to finish a piece. That depends on the size of your pattern. I chose a delicate little snowflake so I wouldn't feel overwhelmed.

When I started my snowflake, I thought, *I'm going to make one of these*

223

for each of my friends and put it on the outside of their Christmas packages. After five hours and a minuscule amount of any noticeable progress, I reconsidered: *I'll give these only to my best friends and include them in their gift boxes.*

A week later, I realized I didn't have a friend worth this kind of effort; only select family members would get these gems—and that would be *all* they'd get. I'd also include a contract for them to agree to display their snowflakes under glass in a heavy traffic area of their homes—all year long.

Fifteen hours into my little winter-wonder project, I decided this would be the first and last paper wad I'd ever make—and I'd keep it for myself.

The greatest use of life is to spend it for something that will outlast it.
WILLIAM JAMES

THANKS
FOR THE PRIVILEGE

JAROLDEEN EDWARDS
FROM *THINGS I WISH I'D KNOWN SOONER*

R ecently while attending some business meetings in Chicago with my husband, I went to a museum with the wife of a prominent mortgage banker. She is a woman whom I admire and like a great deal. She has character, charm, education, wit, and a wonderful sense of self.

Polly was raised in New England and lived there with her husband for many years. Recently she had moved to the Southwest because of her husband's work. With typical flair, good cheer, and optimism, Polly had accepted this upheaval in her life. Almost immediately upon moving, she set herself the task of designing and building a home. When the house was completed, it was a place of warmth and beauty, a contemporary adaptation of a New England colonial, with fireplaces, high ceilings, and a spacious entrance hall—everything designed to welcome and embrace, not to impress. She furnished the home with antiques collected by generations of her family, including a mahogany dining-room set made by her great-grandfather, a New England cabinetmaker.

The home was as charming, appealing, lovely, and impressive as Polly herself. But the thing that made her home unique was the way she put together the open house she held as soon as it was completed. It was a great party, brimming with flowers, food, music, and conversation. Polly invited all of her wide circle of old and new friends, including business associates, neighbors, fellow volunteers from various charity organizations with which she was involved, members of her book club, grocery-store clerks, her doctor and dentist, and many others with whom she came in contact.

Also included in the party were the men who had helped to build the house. These men were the honored guests, from the ditch diggers to the painters, the carpenters, the men who installed the carpets, the plumbers, and the electricians. She knew them all by name, and welcomed them with open arms. As she introduced these people with gratitude and warm affection, Polly commented, "This is really their house, you know. They made it. Without them, it wouldn't exist."

As we rode to the museum that day, Polly and I talked about many things. Assuming that a woman with Polly's resources must be involved in some impressive endeavor, I asked, "Well, now that your new home is finished and your youngest son is off to college, what new challenge are you going to take on?" (I know now how many false assumptions are contained in that question.) Polly sat quietly for a moment, then turned to me with a smile and a slight shrug of her shoulders. What she then said pierced me to the quick. It was a moment of insight that I believe every woman should experience.

"I just want to keep doing the most important thing, the thing that I love above everything else," she said. "I just want to keep finding ways to do it better. All my life, for the rest of my life, I want to keep being the finest wife, the most loving and caring mother—and, I hope, someday, grandmother—it is possible to be. To me, nothing else holds a candle to this in terms of satisfaction and importance. Anything else I do is just my way of saying thank you for the privilege of being a mother."

ICE CREAM

JOE LOMUSIO
FROM *IF I SHOULD DIE BEFORE I LIVE*

A tourist was standing in line to buy an ice cream cone at a Thrifty Drug store in Beverly Hills. To her utter shock and amazement, who should walk in and stand right behind her but Paul Newman! Well the lady, even though she was rattled, determined to maintain her composure. She purchased her ice cream cone and turned confidently and exited the store.

However, to her horror, she realized that she had left the counter without her ice cream cone! She waited a few minutes till she felt all was clear, and then went back into the store to claim her cone. As she approached the counter, the cone was not in the little circular receptacle, and for a moment she stood there pondering what might have happened to it. Then she felt a polite tap on her shoulder, and turning was confronted by—you guessed it—Paul Newman. The famous actor then told the lady that if she was looking for her ice cream cone, she had put it into her purse!

PICTURE PERFECT

ANN CAMPSHURE
FROM VIRTUE MAGAZINE

*J*ust off center in a country scene, an ancient wagon wheel leans against a rotting post. Weedy shrubs threaten to overtake the wildflowers growing near its base, and atop the post rests an old battered mailbox, its door dangling by one rusty hinge.

Inside, nestled in their twiggy haven, four tiny bluebirds wait impatiently for their meal, while their cautious mother perches on the branch of a twisted sapling that juts across the opening of the mailbox.

When I first saw the print at a rummage sale, I was repelled by its unattractive setting.

"Five dollars?" I whispered to my friend Grace. "I wouldn't pay fifty cents for that picture!"

Yet something intrigued me about this scene; I was drawn back for another look.

Peering closer, I realized the mother bluebird had chosen her nesting site with care. In this rundown shell of a house, her babies would be safe and dry while she and her mate looked for food. This tiny homemaker wasn't worried about what the neighbors might think or whether her nest would pass the white glove test.

I couldn't help but compare her outlook on housekeeping with my own. For years I've struggled to find the balance between an unkempt house and unrealistic perfection.

After we remodeled our house about ten years ago, I was determined to keep it looking picture perfect, like a page out of *Better Homes and Gardens*. But it didn't happen.

Our dear old German shepherd continued to shed furry tufts of white hair, which piled up like tiny snowdrifts along the baseboards.

Then there was the new wood-burning stove, which provided cozy warmth but eventually turned our pristine ceiling a sooty white.

And our kids, well, continued to be kids!

One day, after listening to my usual fussing and complaining about the state of our house, my husband finally asked me, "What do you want: a house or a home?" I hate it when he's right, especially when it's something I should have known all along!

His words stayed with me for days. Then I found the bluebird picture, and I believed God was strongly suggesting that I change my attitude and priorities. Overcoming my last remnant of hesitation, I paid the price and took the print home. After dusting its plain wooden frame, I hung the picture where I'd see it daily and be challenged by its simple message: The house does not make the home.

That was years ago, and I wish I could say that I learned my lesson once and for all. But I still occasionally find myself struggling over priorities when it comes to choosing between a clean, tidy house and the needs of my family.

Last Saturday, my ten-year-old granddaughter, Kerri, spent the day at our house. All morning, while I cleaned and did laundry, she busied herself reading, drawing pictures of horses, and converting our spare room into her own private office.

Shortly after lunch, she grew tired of her own company. The kids next door weren't home, Grandpa was still at work, and it was raining outside.

"Grandma, will you play a game with me?" Kerri asked.

Anxious to finish my appointed tasks for the day, I turned down her invitation to play. I needed to get that load of whites folded and put away. On my way to the laundry room, I passed the bluebird picture. It had become so much a part of the room that I hardly took notice of it anymore, but Saturday it caught my attention.

Four tiny pairs of eyes seemed to stare into mine, begging me to reconsider. I could almost hear my husband's pointed question: "What do you want: a house or a home?"

Suddenly I realized that socks and underwear would always need my attention, but someday that little girl may stop asking.

By afternoon's end I had lost several games to my granddaughter and the laundry still lay jumbled in the dryer, but I knew I couldn't have found a better way to use my time.

*Happiness comes from braiding together
what one would like to have and what one has.*

CLARE DELONG

TRAFFIC BALLET

MARILYN MEBERG
FROM *JOY BREAKS*

ood Morning, America interviewed a guy named Tony from Providence, Rhode Island, who is a traffic cop. He described how neither he nor any of the other guys on the traffic detail could bear one duty each of them had for at least an hour a day. They had to stand in the middle of a busy intersection directing traffic, and he said it was so boring and uneventful he could hardly endure it. He decided to try and spice up that dull task with something that would at least entertain himself and make the hour go faster.

He began experimenting with exaggerated hand and arm movements which led to rhythmically syncopated body swings to go with the movements of his limbs. Finally, after only a few days, he began twirling from left to right, startling drivers with his flourishes of "hurry up," "slow down," or "stop!" That ultimately led to occasionally doing full body spins which culminated in the splits.

Motorists grew to appreciate his antics so much they honked and clapped until he had so many enthusiastic fans it created traffic jams, which only increased his need to twirl, flourish, and point to get cars moving. To avoid the hazards his accumulation of fans presented, Tony was assigned to different intersections each day so no one knew for sure where he'd be performing.

As this interview was going on we, the viewing audience, were treated to a video of Tony's "intersection ballet." Buses and cars were whizzing past in such close proximity to him I wondered if he was ever hit by any of the vehicles. The question was posed to Tony, and he said that he bounced off the side of a moving bus once because he lost his balance during one of his twirls. He said he suffered no bodily harm from the experience but that it did inspire him to do a bit of practicing of his twirls in the basement of his home that night.

What a perfect example Tony is of how to practice a laugh lifestyle. A laugh lifestyle is predicated upon our attitude toward the daily stuff of life. When those tasks seem too dull to endure, figure out a way to make them fun; get creative and entertain yourself. If the stuff of life for you right now is not dull and boring but instead painful and overwhelming, find something in the midst of the pain that makes you smile or giggle anyway. There's always something somewhere…even if you have to just pretend to laugh until you really do!

You need that joy break, so take at least one every day. Hey, how about twirling and flourishing in your kitchen, grocery store, or office? It works for Tony!

A PRAYER FOR THOSE GROWING OLDER

AUTHOR UNKNOWN

Lord, Thou knowest that I am growing older.

Keep me from growing talkative and possessed with the idea that I must express myself on every subject.

Release me from the craving to straighten out everyone's affairs.

Keep me from the recital of endless details. Give me wings to get to the point.

Seal my lips when I am inclined to tell of my aches and pains. They are increasing with the years and my love to speak of them grows sweeter as time goes by.

Make me thoughtful but not nosey; helpful but not bossy.

Teach me the glorious lesson that occasionally I may be wrong.

With my vast store of wisdom and experience, it does seem a pity not to use it all. But thou knowest, Lord, that I want a few friends in the end.

BEHIND THE
QUICK SKETCH

JONI EARECKSON TADA
FROM *GLORIOUS INTRUDER*

*M*y art instructor, an excellent craftsman, told me a compelling story about the benefits of diligent work.

Many years ago there was a famous Japanese artist named Hokusai, whose paintings were coveted by royalty. One day a nobleman requested a special painting of his prized bird. He left the bird with Hokusai, and the artist told the nobleman to return in a week.

The master missed his beautiful bird, and was anxious to return at the end of the week not only to secure his favorite pet, but his painting as well. When the nobleman arrived, however, the artist humbly requested a two-week postponement.

The two-week delay stretched into two months—and then six.

A year later, the nobleman stormed into Hokusai's studio. He refused to wait any longer and demanded both his bird and his painting. Hokusai, in the Japanese way, bowed to the nobleman, turned to his workshop table, and picked up a brush and a large sheet of rice paper. Within moments he had effortlessly painted an exact likeness of the lovely bird.

The bird's owner was stunned by the painting.

And then he was angry. "Why did you keep me waiting for a year if you could have done the painting in such a short time?"

"You don't understand," Hokusai replied. Then he escorted the noble-man into a room where the walls were covered with paintings of the same bird. None of them, however, matched the grace and the beauty of the final rendering. Yet, out of such hard work and painstaking effort came the mastery of Hokusai's art.

My art instructor's point was clear. Nothing of real worth or lasting value comes easy.

Today is the tomorrow you worried about yesterday and all is well.

ANONYMOUS

BUNNY SLIPPERS

BARBARA JOHNSON
FROM *MAMA, GET THE HAMMER*

It's healthy to be willing to laugh at yourself and make light of your shortcomings. We all have our quirks, so we shouldn't take ourselves too seriously. One of the best solutions I know for that is to take the "bunny-slipper approach," a philosophy of life we all need to practice.

A friend sent me a pair of bunny slippers, and every now and then I put them on, especially when I'm tempted to start thinking I'm important or "nearly famous." There's something about bunny slippers that keeps my perspective where it belongs, but in addition to that, my bunny slippers remind me that whatever happens doesn't have to get me down. I can still be a little silly and laugh and enjoy life. Pain dissolves, frustrations vanish, and burdens roll away when I have on my bunny slippers.

MORNING SONG

RUTH BELL GRAHAM
FROM *LEGACY OF A PACK RAT*

I had been getting up early, fixing myself a cup of coffee, and then sitting in the rocker on the front porch while I prayed for each of our children, and for each of theirs.

One morning I awoke earlier than usual. It was five o'clock, with dawn just breaking over the mountains. I collected my cup of coffee and settled into the old rocker. Suddenly, I realized a symphony of bird song was literally surrounding me. The air was liquid with music, as if the whole creation were praising God at the beginning of a new day. I chuckled to hear the old turkey gobbler, that had recently joined our family, gobbling away down in the woods at the top of his voice as if he were a song sparrow!

And I learned a lesson. I had been beginning my days with petitions, and I should have been beginning them with praise.

VERNA'S SECRET

LINDA ANDERSEN
FROM *SLICES OF LIFE*

*S*he lives alone in tiny, second-story rooms above a weatherbeaten general store and gas station that have seen better days. No one has used them for years. Verna Bok has been a widow for 40 years, I learned one Sunday after church. This diminutive lady without a car is always in church (when she's well), and she's always smiling. I wondered why as I watched her come and go, leaning heavily on her cane.

The blinds at Verna's windows are slightly askew and the building she lives in looks perpetually deserted and forgotten. A lone gas pump sits stolidly out in front near the road like a paunchy, middle-aged man with nothing much to do except watch the traffic go by. The old, sun-faded pump hasn't served our lazy little community in more years than anyone can remember. The cost of gasoline still reads 31 cents a gallon—just as if inflation never happened—just as if it remembers a time when our tiny farming town boasted enough "live" businesses to keep the main road buzzing with activity. Verna remembers those days well enough. Now business has gone elsewhere, leaving the village of Forest Grove and Verna to grow old together. But Verna Bok is not a person who merely sits still and grows old, as I soon discovered.

I was having some neighbors in one evening, and on a sudden

impulse I decided to include Verna.

"How nice!" she beamed over the telephone wire connecting our voices. "How very nice of you to call. I'd surely come if I was well enough." She had been sick for a couple of weeks up there alone in that tiny apartment. I was sorry, and I told her so.

"You must get awfully lonesome, Verna."

"Lonesome?" She sounded surprised. "Oh my, no," she bubbled, laughing. "Why, I'm never lonesome." (I had a feeling I was about to discover something.) "You see, I have all my good memories to keep me company—and my photograph albums too. And then, 'a course, I keep so busy with Ruth's boys."

"Oh?" I asked, before remembering that she had a nearby neighbor named Ruth.

"Oh yes," she replied. "You see, Ruth has raised them eight boys by herself ever since the divorce, and she works, ya know. So's I fix supper for them boys every night. Yes, I been doin' it for years. It saves her a whole lot of worry and it gives me sumthin' useful to do. Oh, yes, them boys gets me flowers too, on Mother's Day. They're like m'own boys." Now I knew that this was an unusual person indeed. And I began to understand the secret of her youthful exuberance for life.

Verna had learned something that most people take a lifetime to discover, and she had found it less than a country mile from her own home. Without actually looking for happiness, she had kept herself busy filling the empty cups of other people's lives.

When my husband greeted Verna in church one morning some weeks later, he commented on the stunning pair of cardinals he had spotted in our maple trees. "Verna," he emphasized, "they would have knocked your eyes out!" Her warm eyes brightened, and her familiar smile appeared.

"Oh yes," she chuckled. "And you know, I heard the most beautiful wren song just this morning." She shook her finger for emphasis as she talked. "I get up early every day, ya know, so's I don't miss a thing. I like to watch the houses around here wake up, don'tcha know. Yessir, there's so much ta see—so much ta see. And I enjoy everything God has made—

everything, don'tcha see?" The secret was finally out.

Verna, you get up to see what most of us miss, or ignore, or are just too busy to enjoy. You magnify the plusses God places all over your small world. You seem to paint a rainbow around every little event, even the early morning song of a little bird. There's no need to feel sorry for you, Verna. None whatever. You have no time to feel sorry for yourself. You're too busy giving thanks and enjoying things.

Keep it up, Verna. Your sunshiny ways are bringing God's light to a lot of lives—including mine.

Take time to laugh.
It is the music of the soul.
ANONYMOUS

LIFTED

ROCHELLE M. PENNINGTON

*G*ramps was a talker since the day he was born, and at the ripe old age of eightyish, practice had certainly made perfect. Easy-flowing conversations had always kept him in the thick of things; exactly where he liked to be.

His daily rounds led him through town in a predictable manner: post office, café, hardware store, grocery mart—and pretty much in that order. Since he preferred getting his news from people rather than from the papers, this could be accomplished easily enough while "out and about" among the locals. He'd return home midafternoon quite satisfied that he had a handle on the world: what was new, what was old, and what was in between.

Today was not unlike any other day, with Gramps making his final stop at the grocery store to pick up a loaf of bread before heading home. That's when he spotted them: the non-locals. A mother with two small children had just rounded the corner of the aisle. There wasn't anything Gramps enjoyed quite so much as striking up small talk with someone he had never met before. Forgetting that he had been reaching for a loaf of bread, Gramps shifted gears from Grocery Shopper into Public Relations Specialist. The process of de-strangerization took less than eight minutes after which Gramps knew that they had just moved to town, were living on Elm Street in the blue Cape Cod on the corner, were celebrating the father's birthday this afternoon, and had come to purchase a bouquet of balloons for the party. "A birthday party, you say!" Gramps cheerfully exclaimed as he quickly joined into their circle of anticipated excitement. It was a nice place to be.

Always helpful, Gramps walked along with them to the back corner of the store where the helium tank and balloon display were located. A rainbow of colored balloons were chosen, inflated, and tied together with curled ribbons. "Wait till Daddy sees this!" chirped the children's soprano voices.

Both Gramps and the little family were soon ready to check out. Since Mabel's line was open, they filed in: skipping girls in pink dresses first, mother carrying white purse next, Gramps and his bread last of all. Being a mother of seven and the purchaser of many dozen balloon bouquets over the years herself—some of which made it to their intended recipient and most of which simply floated away instead—Mabel felt it her maternal duty to gently share some reminders. "Such wonderful balloons you have! Why, there's so many of them I should think they would just lift the both of you up together like Mary Poppins!" Giggles. "Now you better hang on tight. Real tight. Gramps told me you're on your way to a birthday party. We want those balloons to get there, right?" In response, four chubby little hands clenched the strings even tighter.

Gramps and Mabel shouted departing greetings to the family as they left. "Have fun! Remember to hang on tight! We'll be seeing you soon!" Placing his bread upon the conveyor belt, Gramps continued to watch them through the large wall of windows as they walked outside. No sooner had they gotten beyond the expansive overhang of the building than the clenched hands were opened and the balloons lifted. Gramps wailed, "Oh, no!" as he went darting out the door with the agility of a track star. Upon reaching them he continued to lament, but no one seemed to hear. His words were drowned out by the usual reaction of children in the presence of helium balloons set free: little voices squealing, little hearts laughing, little hands clapping, and little feet jumping for joy as they watched the bouquet dance across the endless sky in freedom. Although a natural reaction—a predictable reaction—these little ones seemed to have an added exuberance. *Ah, youth,* thought Gramps.

Touching their mother's shoulder gently, Gramps was going to offer to spring for the next bouquet. "Too bad about the balloons. They're supposed to be for their father."

Touching Gramps' shoulder gently in return, the young woman responded, "And he'll be receiving them anytime soon now…in heaven."

Never before—or since—has Gramps attended a birthday party quite so splendid.

The secret of happiness is not to do what you like to do,
but to learn to like what you have to do.

KING GEORGE V

Faith

❧

GOD IS ABLE

God is able

God is able to do

God is able to do all

God is able to do all we ask

God is able to do all we ask or think

God is able to do beyond all we ask or think!

ADAPTED FROM EPHESIANS 4:20

JUST BECAUSE
I LOVE YOU

SUZANNE F. DIAZ
FROM *VIRTUE* MAGAZINE

On a beautiful spring day, I took my lunch break outside on a bench under a huge, shady tree. I was alone, but it was nice to leave my workplace and spend some time outside, having a little picnic of one.

Lately I'd been reflecting on the loneliness in my life, several years after a divorce and a major move. I'd finished raising my family alone and was occupied with surviving in the '90s working world. Perhaps that was why I had not met a new mate, someone with whom I could share my life and my love. I'd not really ever entered the arena of singles, which was always dominated by a greater number of women (and young women, at that) than men. I kept very busy with my teenage daughter's activities and visiting my grown children and my new grandson, as well as being involved with my church groups.

At the office there were quite a few married women, who sometimes received flowers at work from their husbands. The arrangements often had notes attached, telling them the flowers were sent "just because I love you." I admired the flowers, but, even more, the sentiments behind them. Unhappily married for many years, I had never become accustomed to receiving anything just because I was loved. I longed for flowers like those and envied those loved women.

At the picnic table, as I started my meal, I felt something fall on my head. It was a blossom on its way down to the grass. I looked up and saw that the huge tree I was sitting under was full of graceful magenta flowers, which hung within fairly easy reach. I hadn't even noticed them, because I hadn't looked up.

I immediately saw that I was being gifted with flowers, beautiful flowers from Someone who loved me. God wasn't going to leave me without my own token of His love! I stood on a low brick ledge and gathered a few low-hanging blossoms. I took them back to my desk, and placed them in a glass jar. It was wonderful to see them as I worked, and to be reminded during the day that God wanted me to have flowers, just because He loved me.

FAITH

F — *Forsaking*
A — *All*
I — *I*
T — *Take*
H — *Him*

THE RED LINOLEUM

MARGARET JENSEN
FROM *A TRIBUTE TO MOMS*

I was going with Papa on a missionary journey!

Mama had packed the box on my lap and with tearful good-byes she waved. Papa cranked up the Model T.

We were off to Birch Hills, Saskatchewan, where Papa pitched a tent.

"Pay attention, Margaret!"

I did!

The farmers stood with their hats in their rough hands to ask God's blessing on the tent meetings. The tent stakes were driven into the ground as Papa announced that someday there would be a church with a steeple rising to the sky!

I listened!

Years later, I realized that not only iron stakes were driven into the soil, but the faithful ones had driven the stakes of their faith into the fabric of the community, and I witnessed four generations of godly people worshipping in a beautiful church.

That was also the summer that I fell in love with the farmer's son.

I was twelve.

I never saw him again because Papa got a "call" to Chicago.

With great excitement he waved the letter. "Mama, Mama look—Chicago!"

Papa loved Chicago, the windy city where he attended the Chicago University. He was a part of the noise and throbbing of a big city. Cows, chickens, manure, planting, and reaping had been a part of his early life—but it was the city that held him.

Mama loved the prairie!

She held the letter from the Logan Square First Norwegian Baptist Church.

"No, this cannot be God's will!"

I was sure thunder would roll from heaven. No one defied Papa!

"Why?" Papa looked at Mama in disbelief.

"Because God would never expect me to give up my red linoleum. It took a long time to save one dollar. God would never expect me to give up my prized possession."

I later realized that the red linoleum was indeed a prized possession. It covered the crack where the wind could blow—also the splinter that made scrubbing a hazard. It was also beauty in a small house, cheerful and warm on a cold winter night. It would blend with the polished stove and white starched curtains that framed sparkling windows. (Mama even had starched curtains in the outhouse.)

It was a thing of beauty when we sat by Mama in the rocking chair while we dipped a sugar lump in Mama's coffee and heard the songs she sang and the stories she told.

It truly was a prized possession.

Papa was quiet. He didn't laugh at "foolishness." He knew Mama.

"Ja," he said. "We must pray."

"Ja," answered Mama. "I will put out the fleece. If someone comes to buy this little house without a sign, and then offers one dollar for the linoleum—then I will know God has spoken!"

"Ja, Mama—so we pray!"

Papa was happy. He was sure God would send Gabriel to get Mama straightened out.

Mama was sure no one would buy a house without a "For Sale" sign. Mama loved the wind on the prairie. This was their own home—a garden—and red linoleum. She felt blessed.

One day a woman stopped to talk with Mama as she tended her garden.

"I'm looking for a little house like this—would you sell it?"

"Oh, no!"

Then Mama remembered.

"Come inside and we'll have a cup of coffee."

While Mama put on the coffeepot, the woman noticed the red linoleum.

"Ja," Mama said, "it is beautiful. I paid a whole dollar for it."

So, it came to pass that Papa rejoiced, Mama was terrified of the gangsters in Chicago, and her five children pressed their noses against the sooty windows to watch their world go by—never to return to the prairies again.

Mama said, "When God has spoken—don't look back."

She didn't know that when she gave up the red linoleum the day would come when she would have wall-to-wall carpet. She didn't know that when she left the scrub board and washtub behind the day would come when she would have a washer and dryer.

When we yield what is our prized possession, God will restore in His time, in His own way.

Mama said, "Don't look back." But, I'm looking back and I see God's faithfulness to each generation.

Seven children and their mates rise up and call Mama "blessed."

THE BIBLE

This book will keep you from sin
Or sin will keep you from this book.

JOHN BUNYAN

TWENTY-FIVE QUESTIONS FOR MARY

MAX LUCADO
FROM *GOD CAME NEAR*

What was it like watching him pray?

How did he respond when he saw other kids giggling during the service at the synagogue?

When he saw a rainbow, did he ever mention a flood?

Did you ever feel awkward teaching him how he created the world?

When he saw a lamb being led to the slaughter, did he act differently?

Did you ever see him with a distant look on his face as if he were listening to someone you couldn't hear?

How did he act at funerals?

Did the thought ever occur to you that the God to whom you were praying was asleep under your own roof?

Did you ever try to count the stars with him…and succeed?

Did he ever come home with a black eye?

How did he act when he got his first haircut?

Did he have any friends by the name of Judas?

Did he do well in school?

Did you ever scold him?

Did he ever have to ask a question about Scripture?

What do you think he thought when he saw a prostitute offering to the highest bidder the body he made?

Did he ever get angry when someone was dishonest with him?

Did you ever catch him pensively looking at the flesh on his own arm while holding a clod of dirt?

Did he ever wake up afraid?

Who was his best friend?

When someone referred to Satan, how did he act?

Did you ever accidentally call him Father?

What did he and his cousin John talk about as kids?

Did his other brothers and sisters understand what was happening?

Did you ever think, *That's God eating my soup?*

NO WASTED PIECES

GIGI GRAHAM TCHIVIDJIAN
FROM *CURRENTS OF THE HEART*

A tourist strolling through a European village stopped to observe a master craftsman of gold filigreed porcelain.

He watched as the craftsman took one of his loveliest pieces, an exquisite vase, and carefully examined it. After a few minutes, a faint smile of satisfaction touched the corners of the artist's mouth.

The workmanship was perfect. The size and form were just right; the artwork, intricate and delicate. Then, to the horror of the tourist, the craftsman picked up a hammer and smashed it into a thousand pieces.

"*Why?*" cried the stunned man when he finally retrieved his breath. "Why did you do that?"

The craftsman looked at the tourist and explained. "You see, my friend," he said, "the value of this vase is not in its perfection. Not in the artwork, not in its form or shape—as lovely as these may be. No, the value lies in the fact that I am now going to put these pieces back together again. With gold!"

So it is with our lives. The value of our lives lies not in our perceived perfections or lack of them…not in what we've done or left undone…not in how hard we've worked…not in our efforts, as sincere as they may be…not in the hope that we'll get a second chance to redeem ourselves.

No, the value of our lives lies in the fact that *God wastes nothing.* He takes all the pieces of our lives, even the imperfect, shattered fragments, and puts them back together again with His blood, which is infinitely more precious than gold.

MAN'S GREATEST NEED

If man's greatest need had been knowledge,
God would have sent us an educator.
If man's greatest need had been physical health,
God would have sent us a doctor.
If man's greatest need had been money,
God would have sent us an entrepreneur.
If man's greatest need had been excitement,
God would have sent us an entertainer.
But man's greatest need was forgiveness,
so God send us a savior.

TIM KIMMEL

ANGELS, PAINTS, AND RUGS

❦

PATSY CLAIRMONT
FROM *NORMAL IS JUST A SETTING ON YOUR DRYER*

I once was persuaded to join a wooden angel craft class. The sample angel done by the instructor (art major) was adorable. Mine (craft minor) looked like an angel that might join a motorcycle gang.

My angel didn't get completed because they ran out of heavenly parts. She had only one wing and was minus her halo. Today, my fallen angel lies at the bottom of a box in my basement, still waiting for her moment to shine. May she rest in peace.

I even took a painting class for credit and received an A. *Finally, something I can succeed in*, I thought. But when I took one of my projects home—a still life of apples in a bowl—my friend thought I had painted a peacock.

I asked the instructor how I had managed to earn an A in her class. "For showing up every week," she responded. She must have had the gift of mercy.

My husband, Les, and I started latch-hooking a rug 25 years ago. We're almost to the halfway point; together we've hooked less than an inch a year and should complete it in the year 2012. You may want to get on our gift list.

When I realize I'm more into ownership than completion, I start to feel guilty. I'm not alone in that. Some kindred spirits could stuff a land-fill with their forsaken artistry.

As I push back one box of crafts to make room for my newest inter-est, I'm thankful God doesn't give up on me—a work in progress—as readily as I do one of my many projects. I can rely on his promise: "He who began a good work in [me] will carry it on to completion until the day of Christ Jesus" (Philippians 1:6).

Hmmmm…that's a great verse. I wonder how it would look in cross-stitch?

Have courage for the great sorrows of life
and patience for the small ones;
and when you have laboriously
accomplished your daily task,
go to sleep in peace.
God is awake.

VICTOR HUGO

THE CHAIR IN THE YARD

ETHEL L. LEWIS

omma and her flowers. I think she could take a stick and make it grow. It wasn't easy to make anything grow in the sands of Southwest Texas except for Johnson grass and careless weeds. But somehow, Momma managed to keep a few flowers alive. Looking back, now, I think I discovered her secret.

We lived on a ranch and if you know anything at all about country living, it's that everyone is up early, milking cows, and doing chores of one kind or another. There's always something to do in the country. There were a few times I woke up before everyone else, that is, everyone except for Momma. I wonder if she ever slept. I would wake up and tip-toe out through the kitchen, out the back door, thinking I was the first up. But as soon as I opened the screen door and stepped outside, I would see Momma, sitting in a wooden chair that she had brought outside, humming hymns and reading her Bible. She would look up at me and smile.

A few years ago I received an urgent call to come home. Momma had suffered a severe heart attack and wasn't expected to live. Daddy had died several years earlier. I called the hospital and the nurse held the phone to her ear. "Momma, I'm on my way to see you. Will you be there when I get there?" I asked. She said, "I'll be here waiting for you." The nurse said she had a beautiful smile on her face. By the time I got there she was much improved and was ready to go home. But her condition would require special attention so I moved back to Texas and moved her in to live with me.

For the next three years, the special bond we had deepened and became more precious with each day. Momma would still sit out on the patio in the early morning hours and read her Bible. Knowing how she loved flowers, I often would surprise her with a plant I ran across that I thought she would enjoy.

As her condition worsened, she was not able to get out of bed to care for the plants and I certainly was not blessed with her natural green thumb. I would try to care for them, doing what she would tell me. But somehow, I think the plants knew my touch was not the same as my mother's. They all lost their blooms and drooped. I struggled and they struggled. Momma would often say, "I hope the Lord lets me work in His garden when I get to heaven." I knew she missed being able to care for the flowers herself.

One cold February day, the Lord came and took Momma to be with Him. We took Momma's earthly frame to that same part of southwest Texas where I grew up. We placed her next to Daddy. After a week, I drove back to my home in Dallas. I was numb with grief but I knew where she was and I could almost hear her saying to me, "I'll be here waiting for you."

When I arrived home, it was cold and I was anxious to start a fire in the fireplace. That's when I remembered. The day Momma died, I had put the flowers out on the patio for some sunshine, intending to take them in at night, just like I had done so often. But in the confusion of funeral arrangements and grief I had forgotten about them. My heart sank. "They'll be all frozen and dead from the cold."

I opened the drapes, dreading dealing with Momma's flowers. But to my surprise, every single plant was overloaded with flowers and blooms.

Limbs were drooping from the weight of so many beautiful flowers.

I laughed and cried at the same time. I knew this was God's way of letting me know that Momma was busy doing what she wanted...working in His garden. And I know that early in the mornings, Momma will be sitting in a chair in heaven's yard, fragrant flowers all around, with a beautiful smile on her face.

A CHILD'S PRAYER

CORRIE TEN BOOM
FROM *CLIPPINGS FROM MY NOTEBOOK*

A mother I met told me that she saw her little boy sitting in a corner of the room, saying, "A-B-C-D-E-F-G…"

"What are you doing?" she asked.

"Mom, you told me I should pray, but I have never prayed in my life and I don't know how. So I gave God the whole alphabet and asked him to make a good prayer of it."

HE MAKES IT
TASTE LIKE TEA

RUTH BELL GRAHAM
FROM *LEGACY OF A PACK RAT*

In one of F. W. Boreham's books, he tells of an old Scottish woman living alone and very poor.

But she carefully tithed what little she had and gave to the church. When unable to attend service, she expected a deacon to drop by and collect her offering. The deacon knew well she could not afford it, but knowing also that she would be deeply offended if he did not collect it, he was careful to stop by.

It was late afternoon one day when he made his visit.

Old Mary was sitting near a window having tea.

"The tithe is on the mantel," she said, greetings over. "Won't ye sit and have a cup of tea?"

The deacon sat, and when Mary passed him his cup, he looked down in surprise and exclaimed:

"Why, Mary! It's only water ye have!"

"Aye!" said old Mary. "But He makes it taste like tea!"

THE FATHER'S PLEASURE

ROBIN JONES GUNN
FROM *MOTHERING BY HEART*

oday the wind invited the children and me outside to chase it. So we did. The trees, like dancing gypsies with jewels in their hair laughed above us as we frolicked down the street. The pockets of my jacket began to fill with autumn treasures, placed there by two sets of small hands.

Returning to the warm house, red-faced and breathless, the children dumped their goodies onto the kitchen table, giddy with the joy of discovery. Along with several twigs and many rocks, Young Ross had bagged a snail's shell—minus one snail. Rachel laid out each of her big, amber-colored leaves, then chose the largest one to use as a fan. I watched them as they arranged and rearranged each acorn, rock, leaf, and twig, preparing their own centerpiece for the table. The children spoke in hushed tones, lost in wonder, mesmerized by a handful of God's trinkets.

It reminded me of when I was young. I would regularly bring home treasures to my mother and scatter them across the kitchen counter. One afternoon her hand passed over the tiny white pebbles and squashed red geraniums extracted from my pockets to stop at a tattered gray feather. I had almost left the spiny thing in the gutter since it appeared broken and useless.

Mom ran her fingers up the feather's tattered sides and turned it toward the kitchen window. Soft hues of sunshine lit the feather, changing it from dull gray to bright silvery-blue as she twirled it between her fingers, a marvelous wonder to my young eyes. An "ordinary" miracle.

With fumbling words I entered my children's moment of wonder and told them how much God dearly treasured them. I wanted them to feel, in that moment, the pleasure of the Father, to understand how He delights in collecting the ordinary of this world and bringing it into the warmth of His kingdom. How His touch can turn the tattered into the dazzling.

Most of all, I wanted my children to know that their young hearts are not trinkets to be played with but are rare, priceless jewels in the hands of the King.

They looked at me with innocent eyes, nonplussed by my intense lecture. Had I once looked at my own mother the same way?

Maybe such eternal truths can't really be taught, I decided. They can only be collected, examined, arranged, rearranged—and finally treasured. And this takes a lifetime of days filled with ordinary miracles.

DORA

SUE DUFFY
FROM MOODY MONTHLY MAGAZINE

I'm calling about the lady in today's paper," I began. "I'd like to volunteer my help."

I didn't often respond to such articles. It was much easier to pause in prayer for the unfortunate and keep reading. But this time the Lord seemed to be saying, "Go."

She was an elderly, nearly blind widow. Her house had no running water, the toilet had fallen through rotted flooring, and the porch was separating from the house. Also, there were rats. A caring neighbor who had discovered the old woman's plight had organized a work force to repair the house, and the newspaper had reported it.

The next morning I was shown into the living room of a house that once had been proud. French doors to the dining room hung on stained walls. Tall windows, a sun room, and two ornate fireplaces spoke admirably of a builder somewhere in the past. Scarred furniture was arrayed with dusty plastic flowers, yellowed doilies, and garish dime store knickknacks.

As I stepped into a bedroom, I almost didn't see her standing against the wall. Unfocused eyes behind thick glasses darted and quivered as if searching for the sense of it all. Short, gray curls hung limp against her pale face. She was bent, her frame thin. Her clothes were torn and stained.

Her name was Dora. She was 79.

I attempted to talk to her, but was suddenly choked with pity. Then God's voice seemed to whisper, *She's my child. Love her. That's why you're here.*

"Dora, would you mind if I came back tomorrow to paint?" I spoke loudly and slowly, as if talking to a deaf half-wit. *What's wrong with me?* I chided myself. An insulting do-gooder was the last thing this woman needed.

"That would be fine with me," she said quietly.

The following day, as I was scraping paint from a high window, I wondered how a person could be so void of resources. *What a pathetic existence,* I was thinking when I heard Dora enter the room.

"Thank you for helping me," she said. "I'm afraid I haven't been able to take very good care of my house." She seemed lucid.

"Well, uh, how long have you lived here?" I asked.

"About thirty-five years."

"I guess the town has changed a lot." A lame attempt at conversation.

"I was reading in the *Wall Street Journal* this morning about the Japanese stock market," she suddenly announced.

"Excuse me?" *What did she say?*

"The Japanese stock market," she continued. "I think it's fascinating to track the rise and fall of economies around the world."

For a moment, I couldn't respond.

"You read the *Wall Street Journal?*" I said incredulously.

"Yes," she replied. "And the *New York Times.* I get them in braille."

I was glad she couldn't see the look on my face. "That's unbeliev...I mean, that's wonderful. I didn't know those papers were offered in braille." I was really thinking, *I can't believe you would have any interest in, let alone understand, the Wall Street Journal.*

"Oh, yes. The Commission for the Blind sends me my choice of books and magazines every month. And one magazine publishes my poetry."

"Publishes your poetry?"

I was off the ladder now. *Who is this person you've brought me to, Lord? What is this all about?*

That day, I focused more on Dora than on my paint brush. It was embarrassing to ask so many questions, to plunge so deeply into her intellect. But she was eager to talk. I don't know when she'd last had someone to talk to.

Dora spoke about the nomadic tribes of the Middle East and the feeding patterns of hummingbirds.

"There's so much to learn about this world," she said. "I try to study something different every day."

She asked me if I liked baseball. Dora never missed a game on the radio and could cite the batting averages of most of the major league players.

"Do you know anything about whooping cough?" she asked later in the day. Then the subject was Russian politics. Knowledge spilled wildly from her mental reservoir.

As I worked, Dora recited her poetry. It was elegant, insightful, and tender.

Void of resources? Is that what I'd thought of this woman? *Too incompetent to care for herself?* True, she couldn't maintain her house. But her knowledge was meticulously tended.

After the work on her house was completed, I couldn't stay away. Dora needed me—for rides to the doctor, fresh fruit from the market, a pilot light out on the oven, a battery for her talking clock, help with her laundry. But in reality, I needed her and her perspective.

Ironic, I thought, *that I could see so much through her blinded eyes.* In her, I saw joy uncompromised by circumstances—a spirit undaunted by the appraisal of others.

When two historic houses in the area were opened for touring, I took Dora to see as much as she could of the rich tapestries and rugs, paintings, antiques, and gardens—not totally blind, she could recognize shapes, patterns, colors.

She sensed the grandeur of the house and absorbed it gratefully. She touched everything. Clad in an assortment of unmatched garments topped by a red and white ski cap, she held my arm as I escorted her from room to room. The stares were relentless. I was glad Dora couldn't see them.

Dora is not sure about Jesus Christ. She has read so many contradictory writings. But our direction from Paul in Colossians is clear: "See to it that no one takes you captive through hollow and deceptive philosophy…" Helping Dora distinguish between deception and truth is a challenge. I pray for God's guidance.

When Dora was recently confined to a nursing home after breaking her hip, I read her *The Hiding Place*. Corrie ten Boom spoke to Dora in ways I couldn't. Dora gasped at the horrors of Nazi cruelty. She moaned for Corrie and Betsy as they struggled to bring the light of Jesus into the darkness of the concentration camp.

It was hard for Dora to believe that the story was true. But later when she heard Corrie ten Boom's voice on a tape I gave her, she exclaimed with surprise, "She *is* real."

There's no tape of the Lord's voice. But as I pray for Dora, I'm confident he will call to her, and she'll exclaim, "You *are* real."

Now I understand the curious urgency to call the number in the newspaper that morning. The Lord could certainly have cared for Dora without me. But what I would have missed if he had.

Do not have your concert first
and tune your instruments afterward.
Begin each day with God.

James Hudson Taylor

COMFORTER

JONI EARECKSON TADA
FROM *GLORIOUS INTRUDER*

A very special grandmother recently told me of an experience with her young granddaughter:

My daughter's call from the hospital emergency room shocked me. My granddaughter Robin, just turned six, had fallen from the high bar at school, severely injuring her mouth. I picked up her sisters from school and spent a hectic, tense afternoon supervising the little ones while awaiting my daughter's return with Robin.

The doctor had taken eight stitches inside her mouth and six on the outside. As the little ones swarmed over their mother, Robin sat squarely in the biggest chair in the living room. Her face puffed almost beyond recognition, her long hair still ropey with dried blood, she looked tiny and forlorn. Still, I approached her cautiously, for Robin is the least demonstrative, most private of children.

"Is there anything you want, darling?" I asked.

She looked me firmly in the eye and said, "I want a hug."

Me too! I thought as I cuddled her on my lap. *But how and whom does an exhausted grandmother ask?* As we rocked gently, the words of Scripture came from John 14:16. "I will pray the Father, and He shall give you another Comforter, that He may abide with you forever."

So I asked, just as simply and plaintively as Robin had asked. And just as simply, I felt His everlasting arms enfold us.

Like that grandmother, we often long to have comforting arms surround us in our weariness, heartache, and confusion.

That's what I love about the Holy Spirit.

Certainly, the Bible names Him as our Counselor. And yes, He is our Intercessor. We're told elsewhere He is our Teacher, Guide, and the Spirit of Truth. He reminds us of everything Jesus has said. He reveals the Father. He even convicts us of sin. He does so many things. But one thing I love most...

He's our Comforter.

If you're hurting today, don't immediately grab the phone to call a friend. Seek the everlasting arms of the Spirit. He is many things, but most importantly to you today, He is your Comforter. He has a ready embrace for hurting little girls, heartsick grandmas, worried daddies...and you, too, by the way.

You say it's been a while since you've sensed that holy hug?

Maybe it's been a while since you asked.

Keep This For Me

Keep this for me."
What child has not said this,
And placed a treasure in his Mother's hand
With strict injunction she should keep it safe
Till he return?
He knows with her it will be safe;
No troubled thought or anxious fear besets his mind.
And off he runs lighthearted to his play.

If children can so trust, why cannot we,
And place our treasures, too, in God's safe hand;
Our hopes, ambitions, needs, and those we love,
Just see them, in His all-embracing care,
And say with joyous heart,
"Keep these for me."

AUTHOR UNKNOWN

RUN, TAMI, RUN

JOHN WILLIAM SMITH
FROM *HUGS FOR THE HEART FOR MOM*

I have a dear friend who lives in Dallas, and he has a daughter who is a very talented runner. The regional cross-country championships were held in my town, and he called to ask if I could pick up his wife from the airport and give her a place to stay while she was there to watch their daughter run. I was delighted to do it and so I found myself on Saturday morning witnessing the Texas Regional Cross-Country Races at Mae Simmons Park. I saw something there—a wonderful, moving thing—a thing of beauty worth telling and retelling.

It was a marvelously bright, clear, cool morning, and hundreds of spectators had gathered on the hillsides to watch. They were mostly family members who had traveled many miles—in some cases, hundreds of miles—to watch just one race. I had no child running, and so I found myself watching those who did. Their faces were intent, their eyes always picking out the only runner they were interested in; and often, when the runners were far away and could not hear their shouts of encouragement, still their lips would move, mouthing the precious, familiar names—and one other word. Sometimes they said the names audibly, but softly, as if for no ears but their own, and yet it seemed that they hoped to be heard.

"Run, Jimmy," they whispered urgently.
"Run, Tracy."
"Run."

The cross-country race is two miles for girls, three for boys. It is a grueling run—physically and mentally exhausting—over hills and rough terrain. There were ten races that morning, beginning with class 1A boys and girls and ending with class 5A boys and girls. Each race had from eighty to one hundred twenty competitors. The course ended where it began, but at times the runners were nearly a half-mile away.

As the class 5A girl's race came to a close, I watched a forty-plus-year-old mother—who was wearing patent leather shoes and a skirt and carrying a purse—run the last hundred yards beside her daughter. She saw no other runners. As she ran awkwardly—her long dark hair coming undone and streaming out behind her, giving no thought to the spectacle she made—she cried, *"Run,* Tami, *run!—Run,* Tami, *run!"* There were hundreds of people crowding in, shouting and screaming, but this mother was determined to be heard. *"Run,* Tami, *run—Run,* Tami, *run,"* she pleaded. The girl had no chance to win, and the voice of her mother, whose heart was bursting with exertion and emotion, was not urging her to win.

She was urging her to finish.

The girl was in trouble. Her muscles were cramping; her breath came in ragged gasps; her stride was broken, faltering; she was in the last stages of weariness—just before collapse. But when she heard her mother's voice, a marvelous transformation took place. She straightened, she found her balance, her bearing, her rhythm; and she finished. She crossed the finish line, turned, and collapsed into the arms of her mother.

They fell down together on the grass and they cried, and then they laughed. They were having the best time together, like there was no one else in the world but them. "God," I thought, "that is so beautiful. Thank you for letting me see that."

As I drove away from Mae Simmons Park, I couldn't get it off my mind. A whole morning of outstanding performances had merged into a single happening. I thought of my own children and of a race they are running—a different and far more important race. A race that requires even greater stamina, courage, and character. I am a spectator in that race also. I have helped them to train, I have pleaded—instructed—threatened—punished—prayed—praised—laughed—and cried. I have even tried to familiarize them with the course. But now the gun is up, and their race has begun, and I am a spectator. My heart is bursting—

I see no other runners.

Sometimes their course takes them far from me, and yet I whisper, "*Run,* children, *run.*" They do not hear, but there is One who does. Occasionally, they grow weary, because the race is long and demands such sacrifice. They witness hypocrisy, and there are many voices that call to them to quit this foolish race, telling them they cannot possibly win. They lose sight of their goal and they falter, stumble—and I cry,

"Run, *children,* run—*Oh God—please* run."

And then they come to the last hundred yards—how I long to be there, to run beside them. "*Run,* Lincoln; *run,* Debbie; *run,* Brendan; *run,* Kristen. What if I am gone, and there is no one to whisper, to shout "*Run*" in their ears? What if Satan convinces them that they are not going to win? What if his great lie—that you must beat the others—causes them to allow defeat to settle over them? What if they lose sight of the great truth—that in this race, it is *finishing* that is the victory. That is why our Lord Jesus said at the last,

"It is finished."

Everything

If you meet me and you forget about me
you have lost nothing of value.
If you meet Jesus Christ and forget about Him
you have lost everything of value.

BECAUSE I CARE

*P*lease take a moment to read out loud the verses written on the next page. Although there are hundreds of verses in the Bible that tell about God's love and His gift of salvation, I chose these from the book of Romans in the New Testament.

I care about what happens to you now, but I care even more about where you will spend eternity. If you have never asked Jesus Christ to be your Savior, please consider inviting Him into your life now.

Many years ago I prayed a simple prayer that went something like this:

Dear Jesus,

I believe You are the Son of God and that You gave Your life as a payment for the sins of mankind. I believe You rose from the dead and You are alive today in heaven preparing a place for those who trust in You.

I have not lived my life in a way that honors You. Please forgive me for my sins and come into my life as Savior and Lord. Help me grow in knowledge and obedience to You.

Thank You for forgiving me. Thank You for coming into my life. Thank You for giving me eternal life. Amen.

If you have sincerely asked Jesus Christ to be your Savior, He will never leave you or forsake you. Nothing—absolutely nothing—will be able to separate you from His love.

God bless you, dear one. I'll look forward to meeting you one day in heaven.

—ALICE GRAY

For all have sinned and fall short of the glory of God.
ROMANS 3:23

For the wages of sin is death, but the gift of God
is eternal life in Christ Jesus our Lord.
ROMANS 6:23

But God demonstrates his own love toward us in this:
While we were still sinners, Christ died for us.
ROMANS 5:8

If you confess with your mouth, "Jesus is Lord," and believe
in your heart that God raised him from the dead, you will be saved.
For it is with your heart that you believe and are justified,
and it is with your mouth that you confess and are saved.
ROMANS 10:9–10

Everyone who calls on the name of the Lord will be saved.
ROMANS 10:13

I am convinced that neither death nor life,
neither angels nor demons,
neither the present nor the future,
nor any powers, neither height nor depth
nor anything else in all creation,
will be able to separate us from the love of God
that is in Christ Jesus our Lord.
ROMANS 8:38–39

If you enjoyed reading
Stories for a Woman's Heart,
I'd like to recommend these releases:

Stories for a Man's Heart
Al and Alice Gray
ISBN 1-57673-479-X
Uplifting and motivational stories every man will enjoy

The Gift for All People
Max Lucado
ISBN 1-57673-464-1
A collection of inspirational stories
and a celebration of God's gift of salvation

A Match Made in Heaven
Susan Wales and Ann Platz
ISBN 1-57673-393-9
True love stories to touch the heart

*All of these books are available, or can be ordered,
at your local bookstore.*

BIBLIOGRAPHY

More than a thousand books and magazines were researched for this collection as well as a review of hundreds of stories sent by friends and readers of the *Stories for the Heart* collection. A diligent search has been made to trace original ownership, and when necessary, permission to reprint has been obtained. If I have overlooked giving proper credit to anyone, please accept my apologies. If you will contact Multnomah Publishers, Inc., Post Office Box 1720, Sisters, Oregon 97759, corrections will be made prior to additional printings.

Notes and acknowledgements are listed by story title in the order they appear in each section of the book. For permission to reprint any of the stories please request permission from the original source listed in the following bibliography. Grateful acknowledgment is made to authors, publishers, and agents who granted permission for reprinting these stories.

FRIENDSHIP

"Morning Walk," author unknown. Quoted from *In the Company of Friends* by Brenda Hunter Ph.D. and Holly Larson (Multnomah Publishers, Inc., Sisters, OR, © 1996).

"Norm and Norma" excerpted from *Values From the Heartland*, by Dr. Bettie B. Youngs, author of 16 books including *Taste Berry Tales.* Used by permission.

"May Basket of Flowers—and Forgiveness" by Sue Dunigan, director of ministry projects for Leadership Ministries, Rimrock, AZ. Printed in *Decision* magazine May 1998 © 1998 Sue Dunigan; published by the Billy Graham Evangelistic Association. Used by permission.

"The Truest of Friends" by Nancy Sullivan Geng. Reprinted with permsission from *Guideposts Magazine.* Copyright © 1998 by Guideposts, Carmel, New York 10512.

"Friends Never Forget" by Beverly Lowrey, *Self* magazine, May 1994. Quoted from *In The Company of Friends,* by Brenda Hunter and Holly Larson, © 1996 (Multnomah Publishers, Inc., Sisters, OR).

"New Friends" by Teri Leinbaugh, freelance writer, Richland, MO. Quoted from *The Christian Reader,* May/June 1992. Used by permission.

"The Front Porch Classroom" from *Front Porch Tales* by Philip Gulley (Multnomah Publishers, Inc., Sisters, OR, © 1997). Used by permission.

"Friendship" by Dinah Marie Mulock Craik. English Novelist, 1826–1887.

"Amy Days" by Lisa Latham Green. Quoted from *Welcome Home* magazine, January 1996. Used by permission.

"Little Mommies Along the Way" © 1998, Casandra Lindell, freelance writer, Portland, OR. Used by permission.

"The Hands of Friends" from *A Burden Shared* by Jane Kirkpatrick (Multnomah Publishers Inc., Sisters, OR, © 1998). Used by permission.

"The Gift of Gab" © 1996, Lynn Rogers Petrak, freelance writer, LaGrange, IL. Used by permission.

"Dial a Friend" Article by Susan Schoenberger, Courtesy of *The Baltimore Sun* magazine. Reprinted with permission from the February 1998 *Reader's Digest.*

"The Song" by Henry Wadsworth Longfellow.

"Moving Day" © 1992, Doris Hier, freelance writer, Kewanee, IL, as printed in *The Christian Reader,* March/April 1992, "Lite Fare." Used by permission.

"The Fine Art of Waving" © Joël Freeman, freelance writer, Thornton, NH. Reprinted from the April 1996 issue of *Country Living,* © 1996 by The Hearst Corporation. Used by permission.

"Surprise in the Park" © 1980, Sara (Candy) DuBose, freelance writer, Montgomery, AL. Used by permission. This story first appeared in *Sunday Digest,* Summer 1980.

"But I Don't Have Anyone!" from *Thanks, Mom, for Everything* © 1997 by Susan Alexander Yates and Allison Yates Gaskins. Published by Servant Publications, Box 8617, Ann Arbor, MI, 48107. Used with permission.

LOVE

"Calling Long Distance" by Barbara Johnson. Taken from WE BRAKE FOR JOY! by Patsy Clairmont, Barbara Johnson, Marilyn Meberg, Luci

Swindoll, Sheila Walsh and Thelma Wells. Copyright © 1998 by Women of Faith, Inc. Used by permission of Zondervan Publishing House.

"In a Cathedral of Fenceposts and Harleys" by Neil Parker, freelance writer, Burnaby, British Columbia, Canada. Used by permission.

"Wedding Plans" by Gayle Urban, freelance writer, Woodbridge, VA. Quoted from *The Christian Reader,* May/June 1994. Used by permission.

"Music of Love" by Corrie Franz Cowart, freelance writer, from Corbett, Oregon, currently residing in Pittsburgh, Pennsylvania. Used by permission. Corrie's profession is modern dance. In addition to teaching she has performed with the Pittsburgh Opera and Wycliffe.

"Martha's Secret Ingredient" by Roy J. Reiman, courtesy of *Reminisce* magazine. Used by permission.

"Love Without a Net" by Charles R. Swindoll. Taken from GROWING STRONG IN THE SEASONS OF LIFE. Copyright © 1983 by Charles R. Swindoll Inc. Used by permission of Zondervan Publishing House.

"The Missing Candelabra" from *Stories I Couldn't Tell While I Was a Pastor* © 1991 Bruce McIver (Word, Inc., Dallas, TX). Used by permission of the author. Bruce McIver was the pastor of the dynamic, growing Wilshire Baptist Church located in the heart of Dallas for 30 years. Now retired, he has an active speaking ministry leading conferences and seminars.

"Life Lessons from Lovebirds" © 1996, Vickie Lynne Agee, freelance writer, Pelham, AL. Used by permission.

"Heroes and Heroines" from *Parables of a Country Parson: Heartwarming Stories of Christian Faith and Life* by William E. Barton, edited by Garth Rosell and Stan Flewelling. (Hendrickson Publishers, Peabody, MA, © 1998). Used by permission.

"Heart of the Matter" quoted from *Grandparenting by Grace* by Irene M. Endicott, Broadman and Holman Publishers.

"The Other Woman" by David Farrell. Universal Press Syndicate. All rights reserved. Used by permission.

"Circle of Love" © 1998, Jeannie S. Williams, freelance writer, Sikeston, MO. Used by permission.

"Just One Kiss!" by Ann Platz and Susan Wales from *A Match Made*

ENCOURAGEMENT

"Like Light Switches" by Gary Smalley and John Trent. Quoted from *Leaving the Light On*, Multnomah Publishers, Inc.

"It's Not My Sport" by Betty J. Johnson, freelance writer, Parker, CO. Used by permission.

"The Most Beautiful Cake" © 1986, Ellen Javernick, freelance writer, Loveland, CO. Used by permission of the author. As printed in *The Christian Reader,* May/June 1987.

"A Star in the Apple" from *Home With a Heart* © 1996 by James Dobson (Tyndale House Publishers, Wheaton, IL). Used by permission of the author.

"Crazy-About-Me Love" taken from *What Every Child Needs* by Elisa Morgan and Carol Kuykendall. Copyright 1997 by M.O.P.S. International. Used by permission of Zondervan Publishing House.

"Talking to My Boys" from *Leaving the Light On* © 1991 John Trent (Multnomah Publishers, Inc., Sisters, OR). Used by permission.

VIRTUE

"Measuring a Life" by Erma Bombeck from *Forever, Erma* © 1996 by the Estate of Erma Bombeck. Used by permission of Andrew McMeel Publishing. All rights reserved.

"Love Notes" from *Everyday Miracles* © 1989 Dale Hanson Bourke (Word, Inc., Dallas, TX). Dale Hansen Bourke, is publisher of Religion News Service and a syndicated columnist. She lives outside Washington, D.C. Used by permission.

"Granny Brand" taken from IN HIS IMAGE by Paul Brand and Philip Yancey. Copyright © 1984 by Paul Brand and Philip Yancey. Used by permission of Zondervan Publishing House.

"Robert's Clothes" from *Straight Talk to Men and Their Wives,* Dr. James Dobson, © 1980, Word Publishing, Nashville, Tennessee. All rights reserved.

"Sowing Love" by Gladys Hunt from *Does Anyone Here Know God?,* Zondervan Publishing House, Grand Rapids, MI, copyright © 1967. Used by permission of the author. Gladys Hunt is the author of *Honey for a Child's Heart* and *Read for Your Life,* both published by Zondervan.

MOTHERHOOD

"The Handprint," author unknown.

"Look at All Those Weeds!" by Cindy Rosene Deadrick, freelance writer, Platte, SD. Fax: 605-337-2614. Used by permission of the author. Reprinted by permission from the May 1998 issue of *Country Living,* © 1998 by The Hearst Corporation.

"The Wish Beneath My Pillow" from *Mothering by Heart* © 1996 by Robin Jones Gunn (Multnomah Publishers, Inc., Sisters, OR). Used by permission.

"Collge-Bound Blessing" by Linda E. Shepherd, from *Love's Little Recipes for Life,* © 1997 by Multnomah Publishers, Inc., Sisters, OR.

"To Whom It May Concern" by Ina Hughs from *A Prayer for Children.* Copyright © 1995 by Ina Hughs. Reprinted by permission of HarperCollins Publishers, Inc.

"When God Created Mothers" from *Forever, Erma* © 1996 by the estate of Erma Bombeck. Universal Press Syndicate. All rights reserved. Used by permission.

"Just the Right Size" by Rev. Morris Chalfant, freelance writer and a minister at College Church of the Nazarene in Bourbonnais, IL.

"Letting Go..." by Linda Andersen, author of three books, *Slices of Life, Love Adds the Chocolate,* and *Irresistible Wifestyles.* Available from the author at: 4097 34th Street, Dorr, MI 49323. Used by permission.

"My Son's Present" © 1998, DaLinda Blevins, mom, daycare owner and freelance writer living in Moorhead, MN. Used by permission.

"The Blessing" by Richard Israel, from an article titled *Four Letters to My Child* written to his daughter Alisa. Found in the *Hadassah Magazine Jewish Parenting Book,* © 1989 by The Free Press, New York, NY.

"Bedtime," author unknown.

"I Was Chosen" from *Thanks, Mom, for Everything* © 1997 Susan Alexander Yates and Allison Yates Gaskins. Published by Servant Publications, Box 8617, Ann Arbor, MI 48107. Used by permission.

"Taking Pictures With My Heart" by Vickey L. Banks, public speaker and freelance writer, Oklahoma City, OK. Vickey is represented by Classervices, Inc., and can be contacted through them at (800) 433-6633. Used by permission.

"A Mother's Prayer" by Angela Thole, freelance writer, Riverside M.O.P.S., Bloomington, MN, mother of three beautiful children. From *What Every Child Needs* (Zondervan Publishing House, Grand Rapids, MI, © 1997). Used by permission of the author.

"The Catcher Nest" © 1989, Ruth Senter. As printed in *Power for Living*, August 20, 1989. Used by permission of the author.

"She Held His Hand" by Carla Muir. Carla Muir is a freelance writer and may be contacted through Yates and Yates Communication Services (714) 285-9540.

MEMORIES

"The Good Times" by Dawn Miller. Reprinted with permission of Pocket Books, a Division of Simon & Schuster, from *The Journal of Callie Wade* by Dawn Miller. Copyright © 1996 by Dawn Miller.

"Remembering" from *The Inspirational Study Bible*, Max Lucado, © 1995, Word Publishing, Nashville, Tennessee. All rights reserved.

"Keepsakes" by Alice Gray, from a seminar on friendship called Keepsakes of the Heart.

"My Grandmother's Shell" by Faith Andrews Bedford, quoted from *The Quiet Center*, © 1997, The Hearst Corporation, New York, NY. Used by permission of *Victoria* magazine and the author. Faith Andrews Bedford is a freelance author living in Tampa, FL.

"Pink Socks and Jewelry Boxes" by Allison Harms, freelance writer, Lake Oswego, OR. Used by permission.

"Snowstorm in Texas" from *Wide My World, Narrow My Bed* © 1992 Luci Swindoll, freelance writer, Palm Desert, CA. Luci Swindoll, Women of Faith Ministries, is the author of many books including *Celebrating Life*. Used by permission.

"Simple Treasures" by Garnet Hunt White, freelance writer, Doniphan, MO. Copyright © 1998. Used by permission.

"My Mom's An R.N." by Marilyn Martyn McAuley, freelance writer, Milwaukie, OR. Copyright © 1998. Used by permission.

"Sister Rosalie" from *Home Town Tales* © 1998 by Philip Gulley (Multnomah Publishers, Inc., Sisters, OR). Used by permission.

"A Ten-Dollar Bill" by Don Haines, freelance writer, Woodbine, MD. Used by permission.

"Back Home" by Emma Stewart, freelance writer, Lanexa, VA. This article first appeared in *SEEK* magazine in 1981. Used by permission.

"The Stitches That Bind" by Linda Sunshine, author of 14 books, New York, NY. From *The Quiet Center* © 1997, The Hearst Corporation, New York, NY. This essay first appeared in *Victoria* magazine. Used by permission of *Victoria* magazine and the author.

"The Rose" by Nancy I. Pamerleau. Nancy Pamerleau is an author, speaker and full-time instructor at Kirtland Community College. She and her husband, John, live in Grayling, Michigan. Used by permission.

"The Christmas Nandina" © 1998, Elizabeth Silance Ballard, freelance writer, Virginia Beach, VA. Used by permission.

"Silver Threads and Golden Needles" by Faith Andrews Bedford © 1998. Quoted from *Mary Engelbreit's Home Companion*. Faith Andrews Bedford is a freelance writer living in Tampa, FL. Used by permission of *Mary Engelbreit's Home Companion* and the author.

LIFE

"Dynamo," author unknown. Quoted from *More of...The Best of Bits & Pieces* © 1997 (the Economics Press, Inc., Fairfield, NJ).

"Margaret and Her Pennies" from *Home Town Tales* © 1998 Philip Gulley (Multnomah Publishers, Inc., Sisters, OR). Used by permission.

"A Story to Live By" by Ann Wells from *The Los Angeles Times*. Used by permission of the Los Angeles Times Syndicate.

"Such As I Have" by Bonnie Shepherd, freelance writer, Monument, CO. Bonnie Shepherd, M.A., is the associate editor of *Focus on the Family* magazine. She is the author of *Gestures of Love* and *A Bridge Called Compassion*. Used by permission.

"Hooked on Crafts" from *Normal Is Just a Setting on Your Dryer* by Patsy Clairmont, a Focus on the Family book published by Tyndale House. Copyright © 1993 by Patsy Clairmont. All rights reserved. International copyright secured. Used by permission.

"Thanks for the Privilege" from *Things I Wish I'd Known Sooner* by

FAITH

"Just Because I Love You" by Suzanne F. Diaz, freelance writer, Claremont, CA. As printed in *Virtue* magazine, June/July 1998. Used by permission of the author.

"The Red Linoleum" by Margaret Jensen from *A Tribute to Moms* © 1997 Ruth Senter and Jori Senter (Multnomah Publishers, Inc., Sisters, OR). Used by permission of Margaret Jensen, author and speaker.

"Twenty-Five Questions for Mary" from *God Came Near* © 1987 Max Lucado (Multnomah Publishers, Inc., Sisters, OR). Used by permission.

"No Wasted Pieces" from *Currents of the Heart* © 1996 Gigi Graham Tchividjian (Multnomah Publishers, Inc., Sisters, OR). Used by permission.

"Man's Greatest Need" by Roy Lessin from DaySpring cards.

"Angels, Paints, and Rugs" from *Normal Is Just a Setting on Your Dryer* by Patsy Clairmont, a Focus on the Family book published by Tyndale House. Copyright © 1993 by Patsy Clairmont. All rights reserved. International copyright secured. Used by permission.

"The Chair in the Yard" by Ethel L. Lewis, freelance writer, Dallas, TX. Used by permission.

"A Child's Prayer" by Corrie ten Boom. Quoted from *Clippings from My Notebook* by Corrie ten Boom. Printed by permission from Thomas Nelson Publishers.

"He Makes It Taste Like Tea" from *Legacy of a Pack Rat* © 1989 Ruth Bell Graham (Thomas Nelson Publishers, Nashville, TN). Used by permission of the author.

"The Father's Pleasure" from *Mothering By Heart* © 1996 Robin Jones Gunn (Multnomah Publishers, Inc., Sisters, OR). Used by permission.

"Dora" by Sue Duffy, freelance writer, Columbia, SC. Used by permission. Originally printed in *Moody Monthly* magazine, May 1993.

"Comforter" from *Glorious Intruder* © 1989 Joni Eareckson Tada (Multnomah Publishers, Inc., Sisters, OR). Used by permission.

"Keep This for Me," author unknown.

"Run, Tami, Run" by John William Smith from *Hugs for the Heart for Mom* (Howard Publishing Co., Inc., West Monroe, LA © 1997). Used by permission.

The Stories for the Heart Series

- More than 5 million sold in series!
- #1-selling Christian stories series!

www.storiesfortheheart.com

The Stories for the Heart Series

compiled by Alice Gray

www.storiesfortheheart.com

Life-changing advice in a quick-to-read format!
LISTS TO LIVE BY

LISTS TO LIVE BY
This treasury of to-the-point inspiration—two hundred lists—is loaded with invaluable insights for wives, husbands, kids, teens, friends, and more. These wide-ranging ideas can change your life!
ISBN 1-57673-478-1

LISTS TO LIVE BY: THE SECOND COLLECTION
You'll get a lift in a hurry as you browse through this treasure-trove of more *Lists to Live By*—with wisdom for home, health, love, life, faith, and successful living.
ISBN 1-57673-685-7

LISTS TO LIVE BY: THE THIRD COLLECTION
Two hundred lists with power wisdom, inspiration, and practical advice. Some will make you reflect. Some will make you smile. Some will move you to action. And some will change your life.
ISBN 1-57673-882-5

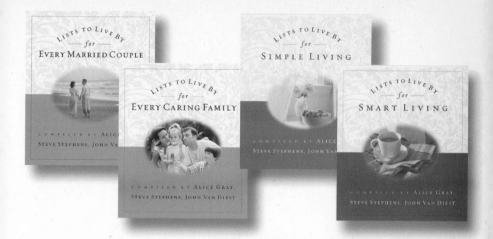

LISTS TO LIVE BY FOR EVERY MARRIED COUPLE

Offers tender, romantic, and wise ways to bring new life to marriage in a popular, easy-to-read format! This special collection of Lists to Live By is filled with gems of inspiration and timeless truths that married couples will treasure for a lifetime.
ISBN 1-57673-998-8

LISTS TO LIVE BY FOR EVERY CARING FAMILY

Provides inspiration on how to love, teach, understand, uplift, and communicate with children in topics such as "Helping Your Child Succeed," "Pray for Your Children," and "Four Ways to Encourage Your Kids." Parents will cherish each nugget of truth in this timeless special collection of Lists to Live By.
ISBN 1-57673-999-6

LISTS TO LIVE BY FOR SIMPLE LIVING

In our fast-paced, complex world, we all are looking for stillness, harmony, gentleness, and peace. The beauty of these eighty thoughtfully chosen lists is that they use simplicity to bring you simplicity—condensing essential information into one-or-two-page lists.
ISBN 1-59052-058-0

LISTS TO LIVE BY FOR SMART LIVING

Reading a list is like having the best parts of a whole book gathered into a few words. Each list is a simple path to a better—smarter—life! If you read them, use them, and live them, you will become successful where it really matters-family, friendship, health, finance, business, wisdom and faith.
ISBN 1-59052-057-2

A Gift for the Heart
Mini Book Series

A GIFT OF COMFORT FOR A HURTING HEART

Consoling a friend becomes easier with this gift book—a small bouquet of uplifting stories to soothe the troubled soul.

ISBN 1-59052-028-9

A GIFT OF LOVE FOR A DAUGHTER'S HEART

From Alice Gray's vast storehouse of award-winning stories, she has lovingly chosen a select few to delight a daughter's heart—complete with touching poetry and charming artwork.

ISBN 1-59052-000-9

A GIFT OF HEAVEN FOR EVERY HEART

Beloved Stories for the Heart compiler Alice Gray offers stories of heavenly hope to inspire the soul that yearns for home.

ISBN 1-59052-024-6

A Gift for the Heart
Mini Book Series

A GIFT OF SUNSHINE
FOR A FRIEND'S HEART

Moments together in the sunshine... Acts of thoughtfulness in dark times... Alice Gray selects stories from her award-winning Stories for the Heart series to honor friendship—that most special kind of love.

ISBN 1-59052-025-4

A GIFT OF SERENITY
FOR A WOMAN'S HEART

These stories carefully selected from Alice Gray's beloved Stories for the Heart series celebrate the peace and beauty of a woman's spirit, with tranquil illustrations and all-new poetry and quotes.

ISBN 1-59052-026-2

A GIFT OF INSPIRATION
FOR A MOTHER'S HEART

Show Mom what she means to you. From poignant to charmingly funny, Alice Gray has selected the all-time best stories and poems to elate and inspire mothers of all ages.

ISBN 1-59052-027-0

Enjoy Reading with Alice Gray from Morning Coffee to Your Afternoon Cup of Tea!

stories compiled by Alice Gray
illustrated by Susan Mink Colclough

QUIET REFLECTIONS JOURNAL
Capture your heart's deepest desires and your unspoken dreams in the pages of this exquisite companion journal, sumptuously illustrated by Susan Mink Colclough. Lightly ruled and graced with inspirational quotes and Scripture...a lovely treasure in tandem with *Quiet Moments and a cup of Tea* and *Morning Coffee and Time Alone*.

QUIET MOMENTS AND A CUP OF TEA
Alice Gray takes you on a quiet journey of faith, hope, and love through stories lavishly illustrated by Susan Mink Colclough. This book will be as cherished as the moments of serenity it offers.

ISBN 1-58860-009-2

MORNING COFFEE AND TIME ALONE
Celebrates the morning and anticipates the blessings of each new day as you curl up with Alice Gray's treasure-trove of inspiring stories, Scriptures, and prose. Bringing bright promise of captured moments alone, this book is gracefully illustrated by the hand of Susan Mink Colclough.

ISBN 1-58860-008-4

ISBN 1-58860-007-6

The Fragrance of Friendship and A Pleasant Place

stories compiled by Alice Gray
illustrated by Katia Andreeva

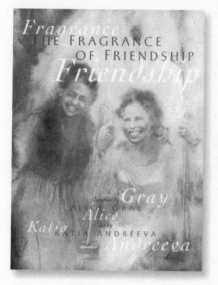

FRIENDS ARE FLOWERS IN THE GARDEN OF LIFE

Katia Andreeva captures the lush beauty of fragrant gardens and the sweetness of the beloved bonds of friendship in this charming collection of inspirational quotes and stories. Compiled by Alice Gray, it encompasses the comfort of lifelong friendships and the joy of those found for the first time...a perfect means to express love to dear ones in your life.

ISBN 1-58860-005-X

PLACES IN THE HEART

Alice Gray's compilation of heartwarming stories of goodness and cheer inspire you to spread some sunshine, like ripples in a pond...and be encouraged in the process. Elegantly illustrated in vivid watercolors by the gifted hand of Katia Andreeva.

ISBN 1-58860-006-8

Gentle Is a Grandmother's Love

stories compiled by Alice Gray

illustrated by Paula Vaughan

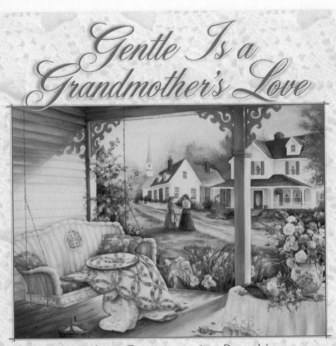

Enjoy the precious influences of a grandmother's love in these touching stories compiled by Alice Gray. Filled with poignant heartwarming moments and enhanced by the lovely artwork of Paula Vaughan, it will be a treasure you'll return to again and again.

ISBN 1-58860-048-3

Stories of Heart & Home

stories compiled by Alice Gray

illustrated by Susan Mink Colclough

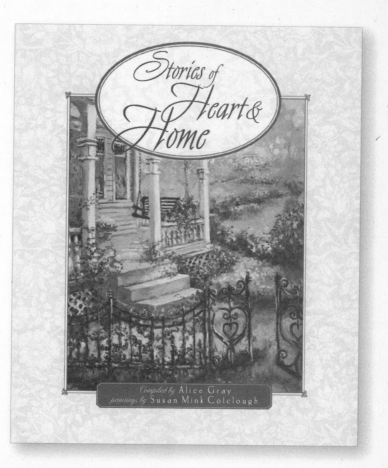

Sink back into the warmth of glowing hearth fires and moments of repose; hear tales of teacups and porch swings and well-used kitchen tables; savor these glimpses of home and let them inspire your own domestic traditions. Beloved Stories for the Heart compiler Alice Gray chose these comforting stories to demonstrate how *today* is infinitely more important than any number of misty, imagined tomorrows—and how the sweet, simple pleasures of home are the real treasures after all.

ISBN 1-57673-948-1

Stories of Christmas Inspiration

ONCE UPON A CHRISTMAS
Compiled by: Alice Gray
Artist: Laurie Snow Hein

Catch the holiday spirit with this heartwarming collection of Christmas stories compiled by Alice Gray. Rich with breathtaking artwork by Laurie Snow Hein, this is a perfect keepsake holiday gift for a friend—or for your own chest of yuletide treasures.

ISBN 1-58860-047-5

CHRISTMAS STORIES FOR THE HEART
Compiled by: Alice Gray
Includes Music CD from
Contemporary Christian Artists

This gift edition of *Christmas Stories for the Heart* offers an uplifting collection of many of the best Christmas stories ever told. Inside you will also find a music CD from leading contemporary Christian artists: Rebecca St. James, Twila Paris, and Steve Green—among many other well-known performers.

ISBN 1-57673-845-0